BEING
10%
BRAVER

Edited by

KEZIAH FEATHERSTONE
VIVIENNE PORRITT

BEING
10%
BRAVER

SAGE Publications Ltd
1 Oliver's Yard
55 City Road
London EC1Y 1SP

CORWIN
A SAGE company
2455 Teller Road
Thousand Oaks, California 91320
(0800)233-9936
www.corwin.com

SAGE Publications India Pvt Ltd
B 1/I 1 Mohan Cooperative Industrial Area
Mathura Road
New Delhi 110 044

SAGE Publications Asia-Pacific Pte Ltd
3 Church Street
#10-04 Samsung Hub
Singapore 049483

Editor: James Clark
Senior assistant editor: Diana Alves
Production editor: Nicola Carrier
Copyeditor: Sharon Cawood
Proofreader: Tom Bedford
Indexer: Adam Pozner
Marketing manager: Dilhara Attygalle
Cover design: Wendy Scott
Typeset by: C&M Digitals (P) Ltd, Chennai, India

CONTENTS

ABOUT THE EDITORS

Keziah Featherstone is a co-founder and a strategic leader for #WomenEd and a member of the Headteachers' Roundtable, a non-political educational think-tank. After 15 years in senior leadership, she currently lives with her husband, daughter, three cats and three pugs in the West Midlands where she is proud to be headteacher of Q3 Academy Tipton, her second headship. Keziah has written English educational resources for Pearson and Teachit, as well as articles for publications such as *tes*, *The Guardian* and *Schools Week*; she also co-edited *10% Braver: Inspiring Women to Lead Education* (SAGE, 2019; with Vivienne Porritt).

Vivienne Porritt is a leadership consultant, working with school and academy trust leaders on impact, vision, strategy, professional learning and development, and leadership, especially women's leadership. Vivienne is the co-editor of *Effective Practices in CPD: Lessons from Schools* (Institute of Education Publications, 2009; with Peter Earley). She is on the editorial board of School Leadership and Management, is a coach and writes for *tes*. Formerly, she was a secondary headteacher, and Director for School Partnerships at UCL Institute of Education, as well as a Chair of Governors in London. Vivienne is delighted to be a Founding Fellow and Vice President of the Chartered College of Teaching. Vivienne is also a co-founder and, joyously, a strategic leader of #WomenEd, and co-edited *10% Braver: Inspiring Women to Lead Education* (SAGE, 2019; with Keziah Featherstone).

ABOUT THE CONTRIBUTORS

Frances Ashton is currently an assistant headteacher (Teaching and Learning) and an SLE specialising in CPD at a school in Oxfordshire. She is also a strategy team member of the MTPT Project and advocates for Family Friendly Schools.

Lacey Austin is an experienced senior leader responsible for teaching, learning and curriculum at a secondary school in Kent. Lacey is also vice chair of governors at a local primary school, and a student at Canterbury Christ Church University.

Jacinta Calzada-Mayronne is currently a special education coordinator for one of the largest charter networks in Washington, DC, USA.

Michelle Cooke is celebrating 25 years of working in the education sector, with two short-term career breaks to support a young family, and an adventurous five-year foray into the aid sector.

Hannah Dalton is an assistant vice principal in a secondary school in South London, and has been teaching humanities in disadvantaged communities for 14 years.

Jules Daulby is a strategic leader for #WomenEd. Jules is a senior leader in an all-through special school in Dorset.

Natalie de Silva is a former headteacher who is now an education consultant working in British and international schools to support other headteachers and help raise standards. She is also a school governor in her local *community*.

Lesley Dolben is an executive principal leading on governance within a large multi-academy trust. She has led schools in disadvantaged areas for more than 20 years. A coach and mentor, she has a particular interest in diversity and inclusion.

Melissa Egri McCauley is currently the assistant principal at a middle school in Pittsburgh, Pennsylvania and has been in education for over ten years. She has always been an advocate for female leadership and will continue to help other women rise!

Clare Erasmus is a middle leader in a secondary school. Clare has helped produce a wellbeing app which won the BETT 2019 IMPACT award; in *connection* with this, she has published a book, *The Mental Health and Wellbeing Handbook for Schools: Transforming Mental Health Support on a Budget* (Jessica Kingsley, 2019) and delivered a TEDx talk. Clare is a #WomenEd network leader in the south-east of England and a member of @WomenEd_Tech.

Alex Fairlamb is an associate assistant headteacher (Teaching and Learning) and a specialist leader in education (History and Teaching and Learning), lead coordinator of @TMHistoryIcons and a lead advocate and subject advocate for EdNorth.

Liz Free is CEO at the International School Rheintal, Switzerland. With headship experience, she also founded the International Leadership Academy. Strategic lead for #WomenEd, Liz is also a global speaker and writer on all things international education and professional learning.

Ruth Golding is a Head of School in south-west England. She specialises in teaching and learning, inclusion and leadership development. She is a coach, a member of @WomenEdEngland and a national leader of @DisabilityEdUK.

Hilary Goldsmith is a school business leader with 16 years' experience across a range of sectors. She is an advocate for the school business leader *community* and is passionate about promoting her profession to better support the leadership of the wider education sector.

Lisa Hannay is an assistant principal in a high school in Calgary, Alberta, Canada and is nearing the 30-year mark of this fabulous leadership journey, being 10% braver as a Strategic Leader of #WomenEd.

Kerry Jordan-Daus is a principal lecturer in the Faculty of Education at Canterbury Christ Church University, UK, currently writing her doctorate on Women Leaders in Education. She lectures in equality and diversity and initial teacher education and is a #WomenEd network leader in the south-east of England

Felicity King is a CPO in Leicestershire, specialising in training and coaching to unlock innate wellbeing and resourcefulness. She is passionate about flexible working and empowering the teaching profession from the inside out.

Beatus Magistra has had a varied career, working in all education phases and a variety of sectors in the UK. Currently, she is very happy working in alternative provision in London.

Kiran Mahil leads Key Stage 4 in an East London school and believes education results in positive *change*. She has taught history and politics for a decade. Before teaching, Kiran worked as a political adviser, with a specialist interest in equality policy.

Sharon McCormack is currently undertaking a PhD scholarship at Monash University in Melbourne, Australia, studying STEM in early childhood education. She has worked extensively within disadvantaged communities for over 30 years as both a teacher and an educational leader in primary schools in Australia. Sharon is a member of the #WomenEd team in Australia.

Fiona McSorley retired in 2017 after 25 years in senior leadership. She worked in a key role training teachers and became a director of a teaching school. Fiona now helps schools, working as an associate for PiXL6 and is a member of the #WomenEd network in London.

Andy Mitchell is an experienced careers advisor, work-related advisor and student mentor, working in secondary and special schools around Birmingham. He previously spent 20 years working in the business sector.

Claire Mitchell is a part-time Executive Head at Latimer Primary School in Leicestershire.

Claire Neaves is a Bristol-based special educational needs coordinator. She has been teaching for more than a decade across primary and secondary, in mainstream and special. She writes about parenting, identity and authenticity.

Dorothy Newbury-Birch is Professor of Alcohol and Public Health Research at Teesside University, where she leads a team of researchers and PhD students. She has a particular interest in co-producing research with practitioners, service users and young people.

Lizana Oberholzer is a senior lecturer in Education, programme lead of the MA Leadership in Education course and principal fellow of the Higher Education Academy. She is a Chartered College of Teaching network lead, a BERA Special Interest Group convenor for teacher education in England and a member of the #WomenEd team in London.

Rachael Paget is Key Stage 3 coordinator for English at Penketh High School in Warrington, part of The *Challenge* Academy Trust. Rachael is interested in improving cultural capital and developing opportunities for students and early career teachers.

Penny Rabiger became director at The Key and, later, head of membership at Challenge Partners. She is currently director of engagement at Lyfta, a chair of governors, a MAT trustee and a co-founder of the BAMEed Network. She previously had a career as a teacher.

Emily Rankin, Ed.S., is a deputy head at The English College in Prague, Czech Republic. She is interning with female leaders in Germany and Minnesota, USA for a superintendency programme and is especially interested in staff development and social justice. Emily is the #WomenEd network leader for the Czech Republic.

Debra Rutley became a headteacher in 2012, at which point her school amalgamated with another alternative provision school in 2015; in 2018, she became the executive headteacher of Aspire, a multi-academy trust (MAT) with four alternative provision schools.

Gemma Sant Benson is an executive head of two primary schools in East London and is part of the executive team of a successful multi-academy trust. Gemma is particularly interested in developing future leaders.

Imogen Senior is a headteacher of a secondary school in the east of England. She has a particular interest in female leadership in faith schools.

Naomi Shenton is a mother to two young daughters and a secondary school assistant principal. She is also an MTPT Project representative.

Emma Turner works part time as a CPD and research lead for Discovery Schools Academy Trust. She is also a *tes* columnist, a founder of NewEd and the author of *Be More Toddler* (John Catt Educational, 2019).

Bukky Yusuf is a science teacher, a senior leader and an educational consultant. She is an ambassador for Leadership Matters, a coach and a network leader for #WomenEd in London as well as BAMEed. Bukky is a co-chair of the EdTech Leadership Group, which supports the government's EdTech strategy, and a member of @WomenEd_Tech.

ACKNOWLEDGEMENTS

Our mission is to empower more women in education to have the choice to progress on their leadership journey. To enable this, we ask women to be 10% braver and our *community* has done just that. We celebrate the brave women in this book for sharing their stories to benefit others on this journey. Countless women are applying for leadership roles and openly sharing their successes and failures to support others. Female educators have gained more *confidence*, as seen in their salary negotiations, the business cases for flexible working conditions, and their determination that leadership must be more representative of the diversity of women in education.

As we write this, we are nearing 40,000 followers on Twitter, have 30 global networks in 19 countries, and 140 volunteer network leaders who are at the core of our *community*. We also celebrated our fifth birthday in May 2020, so thank you to everyone who has contributed to this amazing journey. Due to the Covid-19 lockdown, our celebrations were held online as our *community* couldn't come together in person. It's fitting, in a way, as #WomenEd continues to enjoy its greatest *connection*s on Twitter and other social media platforms of your choice. We are truly amazed at the global growth of this *community* which supports women educators to lead education. Thank you to James Clark and Diana Alves, along with the whole editorial, marketing and production teams at SAGE, whose continued faith in us enabled this book to come into being.

Our acknowledgements in *10% Braver: Inspiring Women Leaders to Lead Education* (SAGE, 2019) concluded with 'Still we Rise'. Our hope, in collaborating with educators across the world, women and men, is that we reach more women who become part of #WomenEd. And now we must all go further. We must inspire and enable women to rise, to influence, to lead and to reshape education so that it is an equitable profession in which every woman is enabled to achieve her aspirations and ambitions.

Still we ALL Rise!

VIVIENNE'S ACKNOWLEDGEMENTS

Vivienne would like to thank Tony and Julie for their constant encouragement, patience and love. My especial thanks to those chapter authors who shared their powerful stories and let me help them focus on the ways they have been 10% braver; it was a joy to do this. #WomenEd helped me to recover from a difficult time and our fifth birthday coincided with five years since my last cancer treatment. Thank you to the wonderful women I have met through #WomenEd: you helped me to see there was light at the end of a dark tunnel.

KEZIAH'S ACKNOWLEDGEMENTS

The privilege of having so many people share their stories and journeys with us is always humbling; thank you to the chapter authors for not only sharing but also redrafting and revising with such good grace and unrelenting determination. Without the love and support of my mum and dad, Andy and Evie, the whole #WomenEd *community*, my amazing Q3 Tipton team and friends such as Emma, Mike and Claire, I wouldn't be able to function, let alone get so far as to co-edit a second book. And a very special thank you to Dr Caroline Badyal who twice was 10% braver herself to believe in me – I hope your retirement is as wonderful as it deserves to be.

ALL ABOUT #WOMENED

GETTING INVOLVED WITH #WOMENED

We hope we have inspired you to engage with #WomenEd, and one of the best ways to do this is to join in an event, whether physical or virtual. Events are posted on our website and shared on our social media sites. Our *community* is also full of prolific blog writers, so have a look at the blogs on our website to see the issues our *community* explores. Our current networks have their own pages on our website, so do join in with your country or regional activity.

Here are some ways you can contact or connect with us:

 Twitter: @WomenEd is our main Twitter account.
Our hashtag is #WomenEd, which we use for all our events and networking so you can engage with what is happening across our global networks. Search for **@WomenEd** on Twitter and a list of our current networks appears.

 Facebook: **facebook.com/womened**

www.   Website: **womened.org**

YouTube:
www.youtube.com/channel/UC_pQlPoWTeKl7MDlDd0-9aA

Instagram: **www.instagram.com/explore/tags/womened**

Newsletter: sign up at
https://mailchi.mp/2eec9d3558fa/womened

Email: **womenedleaders@gmail.com**

PART 1

BRAVER IN THE WORKPLACE

PART

1

1

BEING 10% BRAVER IN HIGHER EDUCATION

Dorothy Newbury-Birch

KEY POINTS

This chapter will show that:

- It was difficult but not impossible to break free of expectations;
- It should be easier to work with small children;
- I took leaps of faith when I wasn't sure what worked for me;
- I have worked with communities to make a difference to people's lives.

INTRODUCTION

I am a 54-year-old married woman with two children and two grandchildren. I come from the Meadow Well Estate in North Tyneside, north-east of England. The Meadow Well Estate is famous for the riots in 1991. It's a deprived area with huge problems and people with huge hearts. I've been told many times during my academic career that I shouldn't tell anyone that I am from the Meadow Well Estate. It's been suggested that coming from a lower working-class area would be bad for my career.

Furthermore, I am loud and opinionated, often seen as a negative for women but a positive for men. In some areas, academia is still very classist and sexist. However, there are people like me who are fighting against this. It's hard, but it's our place to *change* this and pave the way for women now and in the future.

This chapter tells you my story, a woman who worked hard and fought against barriers to become the woman (the professor) I am today.

FROM SCHOOL TO UNIVERSITY

I grew up in the 1970s and 1980s and the expectation was that I would work in an office. In fact, my year group was the final one where boys were automatically offered an interview at Swan Hunters' shipbuilders and girls were offered an interview at the local government pension offices. I didn't take this up; instead, I worked in a wool shop. I married at 18, had my daughter at 21 and was divorced at 22. I suddenly realised that this would be really hard work. I'd grown up in a single-parent family and I knew I didn't want my children to grow up on benefits. I found out the hard way what it was like lying awake at night, often crying, wondering how I would pay the bills and feed my daughter. Little did I know that this would propel me to where I am today.

One day, almost on a whim, I decided that I would go to college to do some GCSEs. I realised that I needed to do something, to be braver, to reach the potential for me and my child:

> 'I was a single parent at the time, and I decided I wanted to go to college because I wanted to be a secretary or work in an office.' (Kelly, 2014, para 7)

This was the day that *changed* my life as a woman, a mother and a role model. It made me stronger and I realised that, although the roads can be long and tough, you can get along them.

I signed up for a GCSE in sociology and was very excited. I clutched the newspaper cutting that reported free childcare places for single parents who wanted to study. In the college, I started asking where I would sign up for this and no one knew. I was getting more frustrated and upset and my 1-year-old daughter was crying in my arms. Eventually I was told that there were no free childcare places. I started to cry, not gently but big, snotty tears and people didn't know what to do. A female lecturer took me into her office, made me a cup of tea and said the words that would *change* my life. She said, 'what are you going to do about it?' This was important – she didn't tell me what to do, she was clear that *I* had to do something. After looking through the telephone directory, I rang the local newspaper who ran the story the next day and, by the end of the day, I had a childcare place and, importantly, they reviewed the whole system for other single parents. This newspaper story was updated in 2014 when I became a professor (Kelly, 2014).

So, I was a college student doing a GCSE. The year after, I did a university access course without knowing what a university was. I just knew I was going to be there. I met my second husband and, by the time I went to Sunderland University to do my degree in social sciences, I was a married mother of two. I missed out on a first by a couple of points, but I had worked so hard and loved my degree.

Then the bombshell: I couldn't get a job. I worked at National Rail Enquiries and applied for jobs at night. I can still say 'Good morning, National Rail Enquiries, how can I help?' in a posh voice. The problem was I had focused on the idea of a job without thinking about what I wanted to do. As Frank Skinner said on 'Desert Island Discs', 'I was running away from something, not running towards something' (Skinner and Young, 2010). Then the most amazing thing happened: I was offered an interview at

Newcastle University for a part-time research assistant job around drug and alcohol use amongst medical students. At the interview, I was asked if I'd like to do the research as a PhD. Of course, I said 'yes' and got the studentship. What I didn't tell my supervisor for two years was that I had no idea what a PhD was. When I got home, I asked my husband if he knew; his reply was 'don't worry, Dot, you just need to write a book'. I thought I could do that and off I went.

What did I learn? I learnt that doing a social sciences PhD in a pharmacology department was hard. I learnt that to do this properly I'd have to treat it as a job and I did – I worked the hours I would expect to work (9am to 5pm, Monday to Friday). Year three was harder and took all seven days to finish, however, by then, I had an idea of what I was doing. I learnt that good friends who also study and those who have no idea about academia are imperative to success. I learnt that I loved it. The support from the *clarity* in which I was involved (at home and in academia) was amazing and helped me succeed.

FROM UNIVERSITY STUDENT TO PROFESSOR

Those 24 years taught me a lot about being a woman, a mother, a role model and an academic. Some members of my family and some friends stopped talking to me as I'd gone against what I should be doing. I should have known that being from Meadow Well came with expectations of what I should and shouldn't do. This was extremely hard for me.

USING #WOMENED'S VALUES

I draw on my learning from this time to shape me as an academic leader and much of the learning relates to #WomenEd's values.

Clarity

When I started in academia, I didn't understand my role; I didn't know what academia was. There were few female role models at that time for me. In hindsight, this enabled me to ask questions at all levels and I suggest we should all ask questions continually, so we understand our situation and environment in both our personal and professional lives. However, over time, I've also learned that it's important to understand the rules that apply to the environment in which we are working. Also, I had to find the right university for me. Teesside University gave me the opportunity to be the professor I wanted to be, to work to my own agenda, with everyone from the vice chancellor to the junior researchers interested in my work. My overall aim is to make *change* at a population level.

Confidence

My *confidence* grew as I climbed the ranks. Others would say that I was always confident and that's been good for me when I was uncertain about decisions I made. *Confidence* (or perceived *confidence*) is fundamental to everything. As a leader, this is the most important thing to pass on to early career researchers.

Communication

One of my main strengths, which has also been identified as a weakness, is that I am heard. I have a voice and I use it. Whilst a student and an early career academic, I attended all conferences, talks and meetings that I could. This enabled me to learn from the best and develop my own style for talking to different groups of people in differing situations. It's my job as a senior academic to ensure my early career researchers and students develop their own voices.

Connection

Evidence shows that statistically significant positive relationships exist between the number of employer contacts, such as careers talks or work experience, a young person experiences in school between 14 and 19 years of age, and their reported *confidence* at the age of 19–24; the likelihood of whether (at 19–24) they are Not in Education or Training (NEET) or non-NEET; and their earnings if salaried (Mann, 2015). I'm now working with my second group of young people from the school I attended. This school was, and is, at the bottom of all league tables. I find this work fascinating and rewarding. The young people choose a research topic and I help them bring it to fruition over two years. The first group wrote a chapter for my book (Newbury-Birch and Allan, 2019).

Collaboration

We are lucky in that researchers don't need to be in the office 9am to 5pm every day. I tell my students and staff that children are a fact and they don't have to make excuses when their children are sick or on holiday. I don't care when my team do their work; it's fine to work at night and during weekends at home. Where possible, we all work at home for the school summer holidays. Plans are made and everyone fits work in around childcare and sunshine. We have a team away-day during the summer to which children are welcome. After the summer, we've all finished a journal article, report or bid which is great.

Challenge

It would have been impossible for me at the beginning of my career to envisage that I would become a professor. Being 10% braver means looking towards the next step; the whole journey is often too scary to start. Take small steps and work as hard as you can today.

Change

I am very scared of *change*; however, it's when I've taken a step off the precipice that great things have happened. An example of this was leaving Newcastle University as a lecturer and joining Teesside University as a professor. This was scary but was the right thing to do. I hadn't realised how ready I was for this *change* and I suggest that *change* is a positive thing. If you're not ready to make the big jump, then make a small *change*; join a strategic group, get involved in writing a journal article or be involved in a bid.

So, what happened to the daughter I had when I started my journey and the one I had along the way? The oldest daughter is now doing her PhD in my team (she knows what a PhD is!) and leading the way for the next generation. The second daughter works for British Airways' cabin crew and is travelling the world doing what she wants to do.

I have learnt that everyone's path is different and leads us to a different ending. I have cried tears of sadness, frustration and happiness writing this chapter. We need to give women the *confidence* and the support to make their own paths by being 10% braver.

Passing on being 10% braver

- As women, let us support each other. Make time to involve other women in the work that you do.
- In academia, long hours are the norm, but they don't have to be. Show a good example by practising what you preach. I'm trying hard to do this.
- Find a female mentor. Don't go for someone who is great in the field but someone with whom you can share experiences easily.
- Be approachable. We all know professors and leaders who are difficult to engage with. Do not be one of those people.

REFERENCES

Kelly, M. (2014) 'How a determined single mum went from the Meadow Well to university professor', *Evening Chronicle*, 23 October [Online]. Available at: www.chroniclelive.co.uk/news/north-east-news/how-determined-single-mum-went-7994868 (accessed 8 October 2019).

Mann, A. (2015) 'It's who you meet: why employer contacts at school make a difference to the employment prospects of young adults', *Education and Employers*, undated [Online]. Available at: www.educationandemployers.org/research/its-who-you-meet-why-employer-contacts-at-school-make-a-difference-to-the-employment-prospects-of-young-adults (accessed 25 January 2020).

Newbury-Birch, D. and Allan, K. E. (2019) *Co-creating and Co-producing Research Evidence: A Guide for Practitioners and Academics in Health, Social Care and Education Settings*. London: Routledge.

Skinner, F. and Young, K. (2010) 'Desert Island Discs', *BBC Radio 4*, 18 June [Online]. Available at: www.bbc.co.uk/programmes/b00sn7dz (accessed 8 October 2019).

2
COFFEE, CALPOL AND CO-HEADSHIP

Claire Mitchell and Emma Turner

KEY POINTS

This chapter will:

- Demonstrate how we managed parenthood and leadership simultaneously, with a little bravery and optimism (and coffee, and Calpol);
- Illustrate how as a school we accommodated new and different models to provide continuity and support leaders who found more traditional, full-time models of leadership unmanageable;
- Champion flexible working in teaching and leadership and aim to prove through our example that it is not only possible but can also bring many benefits to a school;
- Explain how we were 10% braver in asking for *changes* – and getting them.

INTRODUCTION

'[S]uccess is due largely to the good leadership and management provided by the co-headteachers. They work together well as a team and have been instrumental in improving the school.' (Ofsted, 2011: 4)

'As co-headteachers … You have created a culture where adults and pupils make the most of opportunities to improve their learning and skills.' (Ofsted, 2015, paragraph 2)

Looking back, we can confidently say that co-headship is not just a stop-gap solution but a long-term option with many benefits. Co-headship offers a fluid, malleable model as an alternative and more modern approach to leadership. It is perhaps therefore no coincidence that co-headship shares and celebrates so many of the 8C values of #WomenEd. We didn't know it at the time, but, after seven years of shared leadership, we now realise we had lots of '10% braver' moments in our journey, and not just because Ofsted periodically approved the model.

COLLABORATING WITH CONFIDENCE TO BRING ABOUT CHANGE

When our headteacher left mid-year, we were both serving as deputies at our school and neither of us felt in a position to apply as a full-time successor. Emma was starting her journey into IVF, whilst Claire had been teaching for five years and had held the deputy position for less than six months. Back in 2009, the choice between impending maternity or youth and inexperience could have been perceived as a rock and a hard place for a governing body. Any kind of co-headship, even as a temporary fix, was rare. Most headteachers we knew were male, older than us, had been in teaching much longer and, without exception, were full time. The opportunity excited us however and ignited a conversation in which the idea of a co-headship was born.

At a time when headship vacancies were becoming increasingly difficult to fill, the school governors and local authority (LA) willingly accepted the suggestion that we share the school leadership, but what we found were many questions which needed answers in order to proceed: How should we carve up the headship role? What should co-heads be paid? How many votes on the governing body? How would *communication* and accountability work in this scenario? The local authority's payroll had never paid anybody for a head/deputy split role before and the HR department entered into much debate with governors over pay and performance management, and over what would happen if one of us was ill or unable to fulfil the role.

Working together as a *community* invested in finding the best possible outcomes for our school, we found the practicalities were easily solved. However, some of the questions had no answers until we could test them out, and this involved a degree of risk and trust from all parties. We look back now and realise how hugely important the support of our governing body and Leicestershire Local Authority were; as Helena Marsh and Caroline Derbyshire point out, 'In order for the benefits of flexible working to be fully embraced by schools, the attitudes of leaders and governors need to *change*' (2019: 123).

TABLE 2.1 LATIMER PRIMARY SCHOOL HEADSHIP MODELS 2009–2019

- 2009   1 full-time head
- Jan. 2010   2 full-time co-head/deputy contracts (with teaching responsibilities)
- Jan. 2011   1 full-time co-head (to cover maternity leave of Emma)
- May 2011   0.6 co-head + 0.4 acting co-head (to cover maternity leave of Claire)
- Oct. 2011   0.6 co-head + 0.6 co-head (one cross-over day)
- Sept. 2013   0.8 co-head + 0.2 acting co-head (to cover maternity leave of Emma)
- Sept. 2014   0.8 co-head + 0.4 co-head (one cross-over day)

(Continued)

TABLE 2.1 (CONTINUED)

•	Apr. 2016	Acting head (full time to cover maternity leave of both Claire and Emma)
•	Nov. 2016	0.6 co-head + 0.4 acting co-head (to cover Emma's ongoing maternity leave)
•	May 2017	0.6 co-head + 0.4 co-head
•	Sept. 2017 to date	0.6 'executive head' + full-time 'head of school' (new structure after Claire and Emma co-headship ended in 2017)

Our governors and the LA were also 10% braver in taking a punt on two new leaders in a model which, at the time, was not commonplace and raised eyebrows. Our first Ofsted 'Pre-Inspection Briefing', for example, made assumptions that leadership of the school would have been weakened by the *change*s which had taken place, and that assumption required bravery to *challenge*. High-stakes external accountability is often cited as a reason why many people are put off headship (Wiggins, 2016; Turner, 2017), and we can't lie, it scared us. There were very few models in 2011 for either ourselves or the inspectors to draw comparisons with and benchmark against, and therefore we had to justify and prove much in that first inspection.

CHALLENGING THE MOTHERHOOD PENALTY AND COLLABORATING TO BUILD A SUPPORTIVE, MORE INCLUSIVE COMMUNITY

At a more personal level, requesting maternity leave and *change*s to working hours upon return from maternity leave was a 10% braver *challenge* we faced five times between us. One major benefit of the co-headship was that it provided continuity for the school with in-built flexibility. Over ten years, the school's headship model organically *change*d to meet our flexible working requests (as detailed in Table 2.1). None of the *change*s were burdensome, although they did require forward planning, and with support and training the temporary leave windows became regarded as opportunities to retain incredibly talented, key members of staff and further develop the school's senior leadership capacity.

Defying the motherhood penalty was at times an ongoing struggle, however. With each new pregnancy and each new baby came complications – which occasionally had some of our families, friends, colleagues and critics telling us we were trying to do too much and should perhaps be focusing on home life instead. As Jill Berry points out, 'If we *change* ourselves, we *change* the system' (2019: 101). After starting our families, our next 10% braver step was accepting that we could no longer strive for perfection, but instead needed to prioritise a more flexible and balanced approach to work.

Achieving work–life balance is a highly personal equilibrium to find. For us, the answer lay in becoming part-time leaders. Being in school for part of the week meant that lines of *communication* had to be reconsidered and the roles had to be more sharply defined for us to avoid duplication and confusion. There were often times when stakeholders would feel the need to report matters twice and there were differences in our leadership styles which sometimes resulted in 'mixed messages', or at least claims of this. There were also odd times when it was suggested that we might be less committed because of our reduction in hours, or that we were audaciously having our proverbial cake and eating it by daring to submit flexible working requests.

Learning to be part time was initially tough; the arrangement required a degree of flexibility and availability on days off – for example, in emergencies or on those occasions when it was simply easier to call the other party and get a quick answer, rather than delay or double the workload. However, we also had to be strong enough to recognise that we were now being paid for doing less and had to let go too. Learning to draw the line and say no sometimes also required bravery.

Supporting each other as part-time leaders and mothers was so important, but, over the years, our school *community* was evolving with staff who equally wanted to continue maintaining or moving forward in their careers whilst working part time. In 'setting the flexible working tone from the top' (Marsh and Derbyshire, 2019: 123), the co-headship set a positive precedent for staff at the school to be 10% braver and ask for more flexibility themselves.

END OF AN ERA: CONTINUING TO BE 10% BRAVER

Eventually the commute, having three small children and the financial pressure of nursery fees became impractical for Emma. Having the courage to accept this and to end the co-headship, when so much had been achieved and so many had been supportive, required another 10% of being brave. Many women we know in part-time leadership roles or in the upper pay range have shared with us that they can sometimes feel trapped in their current role or school because of the limited portability of part-timeness. There can also be a degree of guilt or a sense of being indebted to an employer who grants flexible working requests. Organisations such as Flexible Teacher Talent (Twitter: @flexteachertalent), Shared Headship Network (Twitter: @sharedheadship), Ginibee (Twitter: @ginibee123) and #WomenEd and partners are working hard to counter this, promoting part-time and flexible working across the system. One of our partners, the Chartered College of Teaching, hosts flexible working case studies curated by #WomenEd (https://chartered.college/flexible-working/). This is a start but there is much work still to be done before flexible and part-time leadership becomes accepted as a standard, legitimate model for schools to adopt.

Ending our co-headship involved entering the unknown once again, as there were simply no models to refer to. It was assumed by many that Claire would take on the role full time; this possibility was strongly considered, but it took further bravery to conclude no, the timing of the opportunity clashed with family need at that point, and instead resignation was offered so that a 'proper', straightforward headship could be reinstated.

It took another two strong women at this point to have the vision and savvy to restructure the school's leadership team in such a way that meant part-time and shared working was still accommodated and championed at headship level, but the roles were no longer co-dependent – which, with hindsight, was a pitfall of the original model. The chair of governors and vice chair gave considerable time and thought to working with the local authority to find a structure where an experienced part-time headteacher could support the professional development of a new, full-time head of school, bringing with it continuity and future-proofing. This unprecedented structure, established in 2017, was the result of two strong women governors being 10% braver themselves. Our governors were resolute that their initial commitment to part-time leadership should continue to be honoured and developed to maintain consistency and growth for the school. They saw the leadership structure as something which had to be addressed, not the staff within it – and they were brave enough to innovate. Other stakeholders, such as parents and staff, who by now were wholly used to the flexible nature of the leadership structure at the school, were happy to accept the new model as another natural progression for the school's leadership. The part-time 'executive head' role which Claire continued with, combined with the new, full-time 'head of school' role, was unblinkingly validated by Ofsted in March 2019, who noted that 'the *change* to headteacher partnership in September 2017 has maintained strong capacity' (Ofsted, 2019), suggesting that flexibility and alternative leadership structures are becoming more readily accepted in the system.

Passing on being 10% braver

- Being part time, having a family or going on maternity leave should not disqualify you from leadership. Leadership can be reshaped and redefined to better meet the needs of modern-day educators and their lifestyles.
- Know when to say no: part-time leadership requires personal balance and bravery.
- Take and make opportunities in leadership: don't be afraid to ask questions, make proposals and point out the benefits of alternative models.
- Courage calls to courage everywhere: our 10% steps in shared headship over the years made for positive *change* at individual, school and local levels. As more colleagues expect and shape flexible leadership opportunities for themselves, long overdue system-level *change* can and will follow.

REFERENCES

Berry, J. (2019) 'Getting the job you dream of: Applying for leadership positions', in V. Porritt and K. Featherstone (eds), *10% Braver: Inspiring Women to Lead Education.* London: Sage, pp. 93–102.

Marsh, H. and Derbyshire, C. (2019) 'Flexing our schools', in V. Porritt and K. Featherstone (eds), *10% Braver: Inspiring Women to Lead Education.* London: Sage, pp. 113–24.

Ofsted (2011) Latimer Primary School Inspection Report, November 2011 [Online]. Available at: https://reports.ofsted.gov.uk/provider/21/119903 (accessed 4 December 2019).

Ofsted (2015) Latimer Primary School Inspection Report, November 2015 [Online]. Available at: https://reports.ofsted.gov.uk/provider/21/119903 (accessed 4 December 2019).

Ofsted (2019) Latimer Primary School Inspection Report, March 2019 [Online]. Available at: https://reports.ofsted.gov.uk/provider/21/119903 (accessed 4 December 2019).

Turner, C. (2017) 'Britain faces headteacher crisis as new research reveals school leaders are leaving profession in droves', *Telegraph*, 27 April. Available at: www.telegraph.co.uk/education/2017/04/27/britain-faces-headteacher-crisis-new-research-reveals-school (accessed 8 April 2020).

Wiggins, K. (2016) 'High-stakes accountability puts deputies off headship, research finds', *Times Education Supplement*. Available at: www.tes.com/news/exclusive-high-stakes-accountability-puts-deputies-headship-research-finds (accessed 8 April 2020).

3
TAKING THE HEAT OUT OF THE MENOPAUSE IN THE WORKPLACE
Michelle Cooke

KEY POINTS

This chapter will:

- Share some of the workplace *challenges* faced by colleagues during the menopause;
- Offer suggestions to individuals dealing with menopause whilst in the workplace;
- Explore strategies for organisations in developing more supportive and inclusive working environments.

INTRODUCTION

There are many songs referring to the process of *change*, but none, most likely, in any way alluding to 'The *Change*', as referred to in hushed tones by many people of my mother's generation. In fact, whilst I am not sure why anyone would write a song about it, I am also very aware that 'The *Change*', or menopause, a natural process in a woman's life, remains largely unmentioned in the workplace.

When I was researching this subject and the experiences of some colleagues, I was met with a range of responses, from the highly encouraging to comments such as, 'Why does it need to be discussed?' and my personal favourite: 'Aren't you worried that if you write about it, it will stop you from getting any other job?' Another colleague felt as if the menopause was considered as more of a 1950s saucy-seaside postcard topic. These are three very good reasons, in my opinion, for sharing experiences and encouraging a wider conversation. There are also broader implications for addressing this. Given that 70% of jobs in the UK education workforce are held by women (Devine and Foley, 2020), if we are to value, retain and develop the workforce, schools need to support colleagues as they experience these challenging times.

SOME FACTS ABOUT MENOPAUSE

On average, the menopause usually occurs between the ages of 45 and 55, with symptoms lasting 4–8 years (Dean, 2018), although 1 in 100 women will experience it before the age of 40. When considering this in relation to the education workforce, 16% of the full-time equivalent teaching workforce are female aged 45–59 (Department for Education, 2019), and, of these, approximately 25% will experience menopause-related symptoms which will have a debilitating effect on their capacity to work (Henpicked, 2017). A survey from the British Menopause Society (2017) found that almost half (45%) of women whose menopause had a strong impact on their lives felt their menopause symptoms had had a negative impact on their work – sobering statistics in a profession that is already facing *challenge*s in recruitment and retention.

However, there is also research to suggest that paid employment can contribute to better physical and psychological health of women during the menopause (Jack et al., 2014). Therefore, creating an environment in which women are able to thrive and professionally develop, whilst accommodating the physical and psychological *challenge*s presented at this stage in life, is critical, if we are to value the wellbeing of, and retain, staff.

The symptoms associated with the menopause (encompassing the peri-menopause and the post-menopause) can be broadly divided into two categories: physical and psychological, although there is evidence to suggest that these do not operate in isolation, and that deterioration in physical health can lead to an altered psychological state.

PHYSICAL SYMPTOMS: A PERSONAL EXPERIENCE

The physical symptoms of the menopause can range from being mildly inconvenient to causing considerable distress. Hot flushes, which in my case appear at the most inconvenient times, such as when I am about to address a large group of people, cause me to become flustered and look confused. Coupled with night-time restlessness, it can lead to the inevitable anxiety of the impact of another night's lost sleep on performance the next day. Some colleagues have reported waking nine or ten times each night, whilst, for others, a night of restful sleep can be completely elusive on a frequent basis. Memory loss can be another side-effect of the menopause. I have become obsessed with writing lists, as well as jotting down the names of students and colleagues, for fear of a blank mind. Sometimes I pretend to know their name, but I find it harder to pretend to remember what the start of my sentence was, which can happen from time to time. There is also now a whole new dimension to choosing work attire, which not only has to look smart and work-appropriate, but will also allow me to reach temperatures hotter than the surface of the sun, without looking as if I have stepped out of a sauna fully clothed. White jeans, which were never my strongest fashion statement, now languish at the bottom of the wardrobe, along with all other light colours, flimsy fabrics, restrictive clothing and generally questionable items of fashion. Even worse, many of my clothes no longer fit, despite my optimism that they will at some point in the future. Poor coordination, as well as muscle ache, can also be a symptom, as I have learnt to my cost, having smashed my third phone in as many months.

For me, these elements have been inconvenient and have, at times, caused me to question my ability to continue to juggle the demands of a busy home life and career. However, for some, these symptoms can be more serious, which can be debilitating and distressing.

PSYCHOLOGICAL SYMPTOMS

The physical symptoms experienced by many also contribute to the psychological symptoms, which can be more subtle but also far more undermining. The following case studies, taken from interviews with three colleagues from previous establishments, give some indication as to the diversity of experience and *challenge*.

Case study 1: A younger teaching colleague, in her early 40s, was diagnosed with depression and found herself unable to express or articulate her concerns about her health. After many battles with doctors, her symptoms were finally recognised as being early menopause-related. She has taken considerable steps to receive support for this, including medication and menopause counselling, helping her to come to terms with her situation and supporting her in embracing holistic therapies. She is still worried about owning up to the situation and finds herself feeling 'inadequate' and 'ashamed'.

Case study 2: A senior colleague, on starting a new leadership position, would go into meetings and burst into tears. Counselling, mindfulness and working partly from home took the stress out of the situation, however she felt unable to share the recognition that this was a natural and temporary *change* in the body, which did not affect her overall ability to perform in this position. After some time and professional support, this colleague now feels successful in her headship and also acts as an advocate for women at this stage in their life and career.

Case study 3: A colleague working across two different establishments was prescribed a course of hormone replacement therapy (HRT) on the first signs of the menopause. This is not an option that is suitable or desirable for everyone; however, in her case, she felt that it shifted her focus away from being concerned about her health, and enabled her to continue to successfully juggle the demands of two jobs and a young family. For her, it remains a private conversation and the *challenge*s that she faces are not something she wishes to openly acknowledge in the workplace.

The psychological side-effects of the menopause are more difficult to quantify and yet can have a far greater impact. Up to 23% (NAMS, 2019) of peri- and post-menopausal women will experience significant incidents of mood swings, in addition to symptoms of anxiety, including tension, nervousness, panic and general memory loss. Griffiths and colleagues (2013), in a UK-based survey of employee attitudes to the menopause, suggested that 40% of women responded that their performance at work was negatively affected by menopause symptoms.

THE POSITIVES

However, it is not all negative. There are reported benefits of the menopause as a time of *change* and refocus for many. Given the *challenges* that can be presented, successfully navigating the transition can lead to increased clarity and *confidence* for some women. Often, the timing of the menopause coincides with other life events, such as children leaving home or the passing of elderly relatives. My colleague in case study 2 felt that the combination of these events, plus the support from a medical team, led her to enter a new phase in life, in which she could realise her priorities and focus more on herself and her health.

Finding the positives can be a *challenge*. However, with a positive frame of mind, access to professional support and an accommodating workplace, some of these *challenges* can be mitigated.

STRATEGIES FOR SCHOOLS

Given the individual and personal nature of the menopause, a one-size-fits-all strategy adopted by schools is unrealistic and would be inappropriate, but there are a number of reasonable adjustments that schools can consider to sensitively accommodate colleagues during this stage of their lives.

Most importantly, a school can nurture an open and supportive culture. Not everyone wants to talk about their experience, but the opportunity, whether through confidential formal line management, or a more informal buddy or advocate system, may help to normalise the conversation and encourage individuals to feel confident during this temporary stage. Having a first point of contact, or wellbeing champion, will support colleagues in developing their *confidence* in addressing their needs. Structurally, schools can look at various policy adjustments to create a more inclusive environment. There is much positive work that is being done by organisations such as the National Education Union and the National Union of Teachers, whilst the Chartered Institute for Professional Development (CIPD) has a wealth of resources to support training in the workplace. Physical adjustments can also have a big impact and it is important to encourage colleagues to identify what will help. This may be something as simple as providing desk fans or adopting a more flexible dress code or ensuring that rooms are well ventilated with options for shading direct sunlight. Allowing reasonable flexibility and support for leaving the classroom for air, a toilet break or to get some water may also benefit some colleagues. This can be difficult to arrange, however it may be that a buddy system can be organised. Some colleagues may have more profound symptoms and may need to negotiate more flexibility in their working practices, which can be done through a supportive line-management structure. There are also various forms of therapy, such as cognitive behaviour therapy (CBT) or online coaching, that individuals may find helpful, and that have the potential to be supported through any school wellbeing funds. Perhaps, most importantly, given the increasing recognition of the *challenges* faced by many colleagues, schools could look to integrate menopause awareness as part of a PSHE programme, so that our future generations can be better prepared.

Passing on being 10% braver

I am lucky to work in an educational establishment that values the importance of staff wellbeing. However, I have also been in schools where any form of 'illness' is perceived as being a personal weakness and not to be 'indulged'. Even in a supportive environment, it can be a difficult topic to address, however there are options that help :

- Identify a member of staff with whom there can be a constructive conversation. This does not have to be part of a formal process, but simply a listening ear that may be able to provide support. There will be a *community* of colleagues who face similar issues and there is strength in *collaboration*.

- Be confident in communicating the *challenges* that are present. Raising awareness of these may go some way towards reducing the anxiety of being misunderstood. It may also present new opportunities as the school becomes more inclusive in its outlook.

- Seek professional support through the medical profession or other forums, such as online counselling. The teaching unions will have guidance for further contacts in this arena.

- *Challenge* the school to become engaged in a wider understanding of this phase of life: it is natural, temporary and to be embraced.

So, at the risk of never getting another job again, I encourage individuals and school leadership teams to embrace the opportunities to create a supportive environment and find solutions, so that all staff feel valued and are able to contribute to the best of their ability. And, who knows, there might even be a song written about it one day!

REFERENCES

British Menopause Society (2017) British Menopause Society Fact Sheet. Available at: www.womens-health-concern.org/wp-content/uploads/2015/01/BMS-Infographic-10-October2017-01C.pdf (accessed January 2020).

Dean, E. (2018) 'Menopause: The challenge of coping at work', *Nursing Standard*, 33(3): 54–6. Available at: https://journals.rcni.com/nursing-standard/feature/menopause-the-challenge-of-coping-at-work-ns.33.3.54.s28/abs (accessed 10 August 2019).

Department for Education (DfE) (2019) School Workforce in England: November 2018. Available at: www.gov.uk/government/statistics/school-workforce-in-england-november-2018 (accessed 2 April 2020).

Devine, B. and Foley, N. (2020) 'Women and the economy', Briefing Paper No. CBP06838, 4 March, House of Commons Library. Available at: https://commonslibrary.parliament.uk/research-briefings/sn06838 (accessed 2 April 2020).

Griffiths, A., MacLennan, S. J. and Hassard, J. (2013) 'Menopause and work: An electronic survey of employees' attitudes in the UK', *Maturitas*, *76*(2): 155–9. Available at: www.maturitas.org/article/S0378-5122(13)00223-5/fulltext (accessed 1 August 2019).

Henpicked (2017) Menopause at Work: Best Practice. Available at: https://menopauseintheworkplace.co.uk/employment-law/avoid-tribunal-over-menopause-discrimination (accessed 10 August 2019).

Jack, G., Pitts, M., Riach, K., Bariola, E., Schapper, J. and Sarrel, P. (2014) Women, Work and the Menopause: Releasing the Potential of Older Professional Women. Available at: https://womenworkandthemenopause.files.wordpress.com/2014/09/women-work-and-the-menopause-final-report.pdf (accessed 10 August 2019).

North American Menopause Society (NAMS) (2019) Depression, Mood Swings, Anxiety. Available at: www.menopause.org/for-women/sexual-health-menopause-online/causes-of-sexual-problems/depression-mood-swings-anxiety (accessed 10 August 2019).

4

LEARNING TO DANCE IN THE RAIN

Clare Erasmus

KEY POINTS

This chapter will:

- Explore how I landed a dream leadership role but then, due to personal circumstances, found myself having to do a 1.5-hour commute each way, for several years;
- Explain the impact of *changed* family circumstances during this period of long commutes;
- Show how I found myself being my household's primary carer and income generator with limited choices, and how I survived.

INTRODUCTION

The first nine years of being a wife, mother and teacher were seamless. My husband would leave at 6.00 am to go to work and I would drop the kids off at school, and then my husband would leave work 'early' to pick up the children so that I could attend after-school meetings. Between us, we would juggle flexible working hours and running the home.

But we do not live our lives as islands, disconnected from others – we are connected to the wider universe through a rich matrix of relationships and extended family, and many of us will encounter the call that will trigger a stormy period in our personal lives. I remember the morning my husband called me to say that his stepfather had died, leaving behind his disabled mother, and he said, 'my mother has always been there for me: I want to be there for her in her final years'.

THE BIG JUGGLE: CAREER, CHILDREN, COMMUTE

We lived in a small two-bedroom house in Surrey and she lived in a large home adapted for her disability in Portsmouth. The obvious answer was that we move down to Portsmouth. There are lots of schools in Portsmouth, I thought; surely I would be able to find the right post? I was 15 years a teacher, leading a large, successful media studies department and was just starting out as one of the country's first designated leads in mental health and wellbeing. I was passionate about leading a culture of mental wellbeing in school, and in 2014 I knew how rare it was to find an academy trust and school willing to appoint me as their director of whole-school mental health and wellbeing.

I did a quick search around Hampshire schools and what I could find in 2014 was only a few schools offering the post of health and wellbeing coordinator, which was without a paid teaching and learning responsibility (TLR), and the media studies head of department post was rare; I was going to have to expand my teaching subjects. Upskilling in my forties was going to be a *challenge*. I was reluctant to lose my leadership roles as I had lost opportunities for leadership consideration during my maternity leave and then returned to work part time.

Ironically, my male counterparts, who also had children, had seen their careers soar ahead – this was something I inherently knew, but where would moaning about the gender imbalance in education leadership get me? Who would listen? I had just clawed back recognition and managed to kick-start my career again. Plus, as my husband was now the primary carer for his mother, my job was now the main income. So, I needed to choose carefully not only for our family income, but also given that my career was at stake.

I would leave at 5.00 am every morning and drive through the hills of Hampshire to get to my school in Surrey. I would try to arrive home by 6.00 pm for dinner. Some nights I made it; many I didn't.

STAYING COMMITTED TO MY BELIEFS AND VALUES

The days were long and I was on the brink of tears for much of the way, with feelings of guilt about not seeing my kids for breakfast or being able to take them to after-school activities. I remember that on one of the earlier trips I thought I was going to crack with guilt and exhaustion, and it was then I said to myself that I could either throw my whole career away and all that I was passionate about or I could have courage, be steadfast and committed to my beliefs and values and test my resilience.

It was then that I started to work smart by using my drives to listen to podcasts that would inspire me to believe that building a culture of mental wellbeing in school was possible, and practising mindfulness to hold me in the moment.

TWITTER AND MY PLAN

One of the shortcomings of being a teacher is that you seldom get to talk to colleagues in your own school, never mind in your wider *community*. Most teachers will recognise the drill – teach 4–6 periods a day; use your non-contact periods for assessment and preparation, lunchtime clubs and duties; attend after-school meetings with a specific agenda; and then everyone bolts to get to their respective families. It can feel like a lonely and isolated profession.

I had topics I wanted to debate; questions I needed answering; research I wanted to engage with, but how? And when? The four walls of my classroom, my corridor for lunchtime duties and my car were where I lived. I knew that much of what I was trialling in terms of research being conducted in my lessons, with the creation of the mental wellbeing app and building structures for a wellbeing zone in our school, was groundbreaking and fresh, but there was no one to connect with and with whom to compare notes and share best practice. I became more desperate than ever for my work portfolios not to fail because I knew what the cost had been to my time with my family.

It was then that a couple of colleagues suggested I find time for Twitter and *bam*! The world literally became my oyster as I remember meeting Vivienne Porritt and Hannah Wilson, and with that I was introduced to the world of #WomenEd.

With my username @cerasmusteach, the four walls of my classroom fell away and the global conversation about teaching, research, mental wellbeing and mental health in schools darted across my Twitter feed; my professional learning network grew exponentially. I started to discover the incredible impact of #WomenEd's eight core values on my world.

CORE VALUES

No longer was I quietly fuming about the gender imbalance and how my male counterparts' careers soared, whilst ours were put back by years as we had children. Now – thanks to research shared by #WomenEd – there was *clarity* in the discussion about statistics, the gender pay gap and the imbalance in the workforce. With the help of Twitter and #WomenEd regional and national meets, I was able to *connect* with an inclusive and interactive female workforce in education and #HeForShe like-minded supporters.

I started to tell my story about my physical dislocation, being the main earner, my son's recent autism diagnosis and my dreams and aspirations at work; about my passion for a culture of mental wellbeing and a more equitable and inclusive curriculum. The *community* listened and rallied around me and I around others. I had often felt like a middle leader who was of no interest to others, but now I was meeting amazing female headteachers and CEOs who were interested in me and my journey. These women were rallying around me, giving me *confidence* in my leadership qualities and encouraging me to take more opportunities to be 10% braver. I was put in touch with people in other schools in England and internationally so I could enhance *collaboration* and share experiences. I was able to create some wonderful personal messaging threads where I have befriended some truly beautiful educators who have supported me through my struggle with the commute; my confusion with working out what is best for my son with Asperger's Syndrome; and my anguish, in the last few years, over my husband's diagnosis, losing his kidneys and having to dialyse every day.

Incredibly, just when I had so little time for all else thanks to #WomenEd, I was becoming more reflective about how I was reacting to turbulence, working out how to drive *change* through that turbulence, and how to be more authentic about my situation and own my vulnerability.

LEARNING TO DANCE IN THE RAIN

It's ironic that when I was going through the most challenging years of my life, it turns out that my life was being enriched. Accepting coaching and mentoring from #WomenEd school leaders was one of the best steps I made. The conversations with them validated my concerns; heard my fears without seeing them as a weakness; coached me through my vision and values; *challenge*d me to be 10% braver in taking the next steps; held me in my moments of low self-esteem; built me up with *confidence* in my ability to navigate my path; and encouraged and inspired me to believe in my role as an everyday authentic leader.

I have since moved schools to at least the same county as where I live, and my commute is now reduced to 50 minutes a day with my sights set on relocating to the town of my school. I will soon be cycling to work. I currently line-manage five academic departments and am still the designated lead for mental health. I work for a wonderful #HeForShe school leader who values me and my contribution to the school. I have delivered multiple keynote speeches at national conferences, have written a book, *The Mental Health and Wellbeing Handbook for Schools: Transforming mental health on a budget*, and delivered a TEDx talk on #familyMH5aday with my daughter. I have been invited to write and deliver training material with the Carnegie School of Mental Health and I also helped project-manage the 2019 Bett Award-winning mental health and wellbeing app – *Brighton Hill Teenmind*.

Passing on being 10% braver

- We will all face *storms* in our lives: don't shy away or give up. Instead, seize the moment of finding new ways of living in the present and 'learning to dance in the rain'. Become more reflective about how you are reacting to challenging storms and work out how to drive *change* through the turbulence. Stay focused on your values and what matters. As I said in a #WomenEd workshop at the 2019 unconference, *Find the Malala and Greta in yourself. Be 10% braver.*

- When faced with insurmountable obstacles, *lean in* to the #WomenEd tribe; your authentic narrative will resonate with many and you will find a support network more nurturing and empowering than any CPD or self-help group.

- Take care of your own mental wellbeing. As my 9-year-old daughter said in her TEDx talk with me, 'Take care of your mind and body 'they are the only two spaces you have to live in'. Watch out for the signs and take positive steps to preserve your own mental health. You are so worth it!

5
DYNAMIC PART-TIME LEADERSHIP

Frances Ashton

KEY POINTS

This chapter will:

- Explain how opportunities to progress in my professional life appeared when I was starting to build my family;
- Describe how the chance to move into senior leadership arrived when I was working part time, and wanted to remain so;
- Explain how I had to carve out what a part-time senior leadership role looked like without an existing roadmap to follow;
- Show how I wanted to inspire and lead whole-school priorities, when sometimes I wasn't even in the building.

INTRODUCTION

'If you don't get out there and define yourself, you'll be quickly and inaccurately defined by others.' (Michelle Obama, 2019: 285)

Worryingly, for many schools the term part-time leadership stubbornly remains an oxymoron. Whilst bold leadership struts purposefully with power, influence and visibility, its poor relation part-time cowers apologetically in the shadows. Whilst leadership propels you onto an upward career trajectory, part-time has you edging your way out: distancing yourself from responsibility and influence; counting down the hours.

These connotations are more than semantics; they feed into lazy stereotypes which cast part-time teachers as the timetabler's nightmare; the CPD avoider; the split class causing nuisance. Stereotypes like these are damaging; steeped in narrow views about the omnipresent leader, they can erode self-worth and segregate part-time staff. In fact, until I *challenged* it, you wouldn't have found me at the top of my school's alphabetical staff directory. You would have been forgiven for thinking I'd been omitted entirely until you hit the end of the alphabet and alighted on a different section: 'Part-time teachers.' Designed to be a helpful way of saying 'these teachers aren't here all the time' the unintentional implication about the value of these teachers is dangerous. It can lead to part-time teachers being thought of as less ambitious or less committed.

We need to think that part-timers are only different in that they work fewer days. Looked at in these terms, there needn't be any reason why a gifted teacher should find it difficult to progress professionally whilst working part time, but research cited by The Policy Exchange suggests otherwise, with 27% of all teachers leaving the profession being women aged 30–39 (Simons, 2016: 17). Progression into senior leadership also seems a barrier, with only 6% of assistant headteachers and only 3% of headteachers working part time (Turbert 2017). And if you have to *see* it to *be* it, these statistics have stark repercussions.

For the past five years, I have worked part-time, first 0.6 (three days), then 0.8 (four days), and I have had two maternity leaves. This has simultaneously been the most successful chapter of my career, with two significant promotions, the second one taking me into SLT and my designation as a Specialist Leader in Education. What I have learnt is that this narrative is not common and runs against societal expectations. Whilst it was obvious to me that I would keep progressing professionally whilst working part time, I found myself justifying this to others. I had to be my own fiercest advocate and refuse to apologise for my ambition because, when there are questions about the feasibility of part-time leadership, it is crucial to 'know … your own worth and the value you bring to the role' (Porritt, 2019).

And that is why this chapter is about being a *dynamic* part-time leader. Because it's time to start thinking beyond feasibility and to explore how you can inspire and have impact. Being dynamic is about pacing yourself: building to moments of leadership crescendo, having influence that echoes and carving moments of stillness.

When schools don't realise the wider-ranging benefits of flexible leadership, they run the risk of losing talented female leaders. And it is disheartening that web searches for part-time leadership garner questions steeped in caution, negativity and fear. Can I be a part-time leader? Is it possible to move into SLT part time? Put simply: you can, you should and hopefully this chapter will help you feel *at least* 10% braver to try.

'PRESENCE IN ABSENCE': THE VALUE OF COMMUNICATION

Although there is pressure to 'perpetuate the myth of the hero leader' (Heale, 2019), it is more productive to champion your part-time identity, safe in the knowledge that vulnerable leaders bring themselves to work. They are human first and leaders second (Heale, 2019). In owning your part-time identity, you can become a role model for contentment not perfection; efficient and impactful but well rounded: the perfect antidote to the rampant obsession with presenteeism.

It is important to have a clear and recognisable vision and presence, even in absence: the illusion of professional omnipresence. Even when you aren't at your desk, your voice should be heard, your priorities must drive forwards. The most important thing here is owning your agenda, and happily there are some quick-win ways to do this:

- *Clarity around availability*: use your email signature to clearly state your working days to champion your part-time status;
- *Contributing from afar*: our SLT meet on a Friday morning to review the week, but this is a non-working day for me. If I have anything to share, I send it in. You might be part time, but that doesn't mean your views don't count;
- *The road map*: a clear template document, summarising what is coming up in that week and what needs to be achieved, ensures *clarity* for all;
- *Sharing good news*: a bi-termly newsletter for all teaching staff which summarises the work your team has been doing can be invaluable. I curate a Teaching and Learning newsletter which summarises the progress we have made against key priorities; gives suggested reading; reviews blogs and highlights upcoming events;
- *Purposeful scheduling*: arranging 1:1 meetings with those you most need to meet ahead of time makes sure that you will give this important facet of leadership the time it needs;
- *Owning the agenda*: ensure agendas are highly focused. Keep to a clear remit: what has been achieved? What is next? What feedback do you need?

TIME WAITS FOR NO (PART-TIME) LEADER

Even when you have worked to create the aforementioned 'presence in absence', the reality remains that you do have fewer hours at your disposal. For this reason, there is always the danger that part-time work can bleed into the hours beyond your paid, contracted remit and this is often a fear which deters people from pursuing it. Surely, I'll just end up working full time for less money?

The strategies which prevent this are not unique to part-time leadership, but they are forced into sharper focus. I have found that navigating motherhood and leadership has made me blisteringly efficient: I cannot afford to tinker, procrastinate or reinvent an already highly effective wheel. Committed as all teachers are, we must prioritise wellbeing by concentrating on the work that pays dividends.

Asking evaluative questions about your work can help: what impact will this have? It is critical that we base decisions about our work on intended impact, and developing effective working strategies for managing time is crucial:

- Start every week with a clear hierarchy of what needs to be done. Carefully evaluate each in terms of time and impact to create a hierarchy.
- Plot in the 'immoveable' and any part-time related boundaries (school pick-up etc.). It is important to maintain a blended schedule.

- Schedule specific work in the remaining time to limit the risk of meandering ineffectually between priorities.
- The working week is not predictable and sometimes you will need to move things around. Do so in acceptance of things beyond your control and knowing that sometimes 'perfection is the enemy' (Sandberg, 2017: 133).
- The meeting versus email paradigm: work to avoid the wrong *communication* forum being used for your purpose. Keep the focus and purpose clear.

PLAYING IT FORWARD: THE LEGACY OF PART-TIME LEADERSHIP

If you are in a part-time leadership position or aspire to it, becoming an advocate for its benefits by challenging practices which limit its likelihood is crucial, and I have found that there are two main ways to develop culture and win hearts and minds over to its value.

The first is reviewing and recalibrating the very policy documents which proudly declare 'this is how we do things here': a school's cultural infrastructure. Whether it is shared parental leave, flexible working, reasonable and effective marking policies or approaches to timetabling, these policies are integral to shaping what Emma Sheppard, founder of the MTPT Project, calls 'family-friendly schools' (Ashton, 2018).

The symbolic acts are about weaving the triumphs that happen outside of school into the fabric of the school's culture. For too long, the concept of the professional mask has been misinterpreted with teachers feeling like they need to completely separate their private and professional lives. Parents often bear the brunt, feeling pressured to acclimatise quickly during an emotional and logistically challenging period. A school which understands life's peaks and troughs is the perfect antidote to 'the premium our culture places on perfection at home and at work' (Ferrante, 2018: n.p.). In the midst of a retention crisis, it could help to give 'teachers a career worth having' (Allen and Sims, 2017: 7) by supporting a more diverse model of what ambition looks like. Cultural pessimism risks becoming a self-fulfilling prophecy, something Michelle Obama (2018: 43) describes when she explains: 'failure is a feeling long before it becomes an actual result. It's vulnerability that breeds with self-doubt and then is escalated, often deliberately, by fear' (2019: 43).

The benefits to retention, wellbeing and cognitive diversity for teaching are clear, but just as important is the chance to interrupt this self-doubt spiral and inspire others to take their next steps in a leadership role which offers them the fulfilment they deserve.

Passing on being 10% braver

- Be the *change: challenge* policy and celebrate your part-time identity to help shift culture.
- Forge *communication* channels which help you share your vision, even when you aren't in the building.
- Hone impactful and life-friendly time-management skills.
- Look to the future: how can part-time leadership help develop others and create a legacy of diverse leadership models?

REFERENCES

Allen, R. and Sims, S. (2017) Improving Science Teacher Retention: do National STEM Learning Network professional development courses keep science teachers in the classroom? [Online]. Available at https://wellcome.ac.uk/sites/default/files/science-teacher-retention.pdf (accessed 30 July 2020).

Ashton, F. (2018) On nailing our colours to the mast [Online]. Available at www.mtpt.org.uk/family-friendly-schools/on-nailing-our-colours-to-the-mast/ (accessed 30 July, 2020).

Ferrante, M. (2018) The Pressure is Real [Online]. Available at: www.forbes.com/sites/marybethferrante/2018/08/27/the-pressure-is-real-for-working-mothers (accessed 11 August 2019).

Heale, J. (2019) TED talk: The Courage to be Vulnerable [Online]. Available at: www.ted.com/talks/james_heale_the_courage_to_be_vulnerable_lifting_the_mask_on_leadership (accessed 10 August 2019).

Obama, M. (2019) *Becoming*. London: Viking.

Porritt, V. (2019) 'How to negotiate a higher salary as a teacher', *tes* [Online]. Available at: www.tes.com/news/pay-interview-how-negotiate-higher-salary-teacher (accessed 13 August 2019).

Sandberg, S. (2017) *Lean In: Women, Work, and the Will to Lead*. London: WH Allen.

Simons, J. (2016) Policy Exchange: The Importance of Teachers – A collection of essays on teacher recruitment and retention [Online]. Available at: https://policyexchange.org.uk/wp-content/uploads/2016/09/the-Importance-of-Teachers.pdf (accessed 10 August 2019).

Turbert, H. (2017) How flexible working and job-shares could change school leadership [Online]. Available at www.ambition.org.uk/blog/how-flexible-working-and-job-shares-could-change-school-leadership/ (accessed 30 July 2020).

6
MAKING MIDDLE LEADERSHIP COUNT
Emily Rankin

KEY POINTS

This chapter will:

- Share how I left the safety of paper-pushing and now aim to lead with dynamism;
- Discuss how I learned to wed vision and culture with systems and accountability;
- Explore the conditions I needed to flourish as a middle leader.

INTRODUCTION

This chapter provides guidance for both middle and senior leaders on how to galvanise effectual middle leadership. It's also my own 10% braver story, as I've served at both levels of leadership and have worked to overcome personal idiosyncrasies, such as feeling the need to apologise for (gasp!) disagreeing with someone or being risk-averse to the extent that I overcook poultry to a grey polymer. The following details practical tips for being an effective middle leader, as well as challenging senior leaders to empower this incredibly valuable group of people.

THE STUFF OF LOFTY METAPHORS

Middle leaders: they're the 'engine room' of the school (Toop, 2013, paragraph 3) and the 'heart of the action' (Rogers, 2018, paragraph 2), not to mention the 'cogs in the system that keep schools ticking over on a daily basis' (Solly, 2013). It's no wonder middle leaders have so many industrious metaphors ascribed to them; their work is critical to school success. However, in my first middle leader post I wasn't much more than an administrator of paperwork; my metaphor was more like a box file. I'm an organised person, so I felt comfortable with schedules and documentation, but I was also afraid of rocking the boat, so hiding in logistics was an (unintended) avoidance tactic.

This shifted for me thanks to two things, the first being a *change* of school that resulted in me working with two egalitarian senior leaders who gave me the most candid feedback I'd ever heard, in a thoughtful and human manner. I learned to have difficult conversations and advocate unapologetically for students' needs. This was crucial, as Women in the Workplace research has shown that female employees tend to get less-frequent and lower-quality feedback from employers (McKinsey & Co., 2016). I hadn't been told before to speak my truth in meetings and to frame my comments more strongly, without hedging, a common female trait and one akin to my Midwest American roots. The second catalyst was an educational leadership programme at the University of St. Thomas in St. Paul, Minnesota, USA, which taught me about managing *change* effectively in schools and the importance of having a professional network, which led me eventually to #WomenEd. Thus, meek box file me began to transition into a more confident and connected thinker and doer.

When done well, the middle leader role is complex, requiring one to be a driver of excellent teaching and learning, a visionary, a conflict resolver, a resource manager, a liaison, and more. For these aspects to be in concert, conditions that allow middle leaders to have autonomy and continually evolve are needed. Thankfully, I moved from the static safety of paper-pushing to be a trusted, strategic cog. I cultivated relationships. I asked challenging questions about curricula, data and expectations, which significantly improved student outcomes in English and Drama. I championed Appreciative Inquiry, a strengths-based approach to organisational *change*, in order to shift school culture towards *collaboration* and continuing professional development (CPD). I saw myself as being key to school efficacy.

Former headteacher Jill Berry (2019) advises in her blog that middle leaders 'require both support and *challenge*, their leadership skills must be developed and effectively deployed, and they need to be listened to and their expertise valued'. Now that I am a deputy head, I strive to do just this.

MIDDLE LEADER MUSTS

Clarify and reiterate your team's 'why'; it will serve as a lodestar for your work

Once this *clarity* is in place, it's easier to strategise how you'll accomplish your aims. When I was appointed to lead Teaching and Learning (TL), my skilful team established a mission from the outset: to celebrate, support and enhance our TL. The idea that we'd get the whole staff on board with the cross-curricular, inquiry-based programme we'd proposed seemed daunting at first. Nonetheless, the mission we reiterated at every chance set our tone, which was one of appreciation and agency rather than criticism, and helped us keep our resolve whilst moving forward. Today, inquiry and *collaboration* are now part of the fabric of our school.

Execute the vision with careful planning, evaluation and oversight

A strategic development plan is an absolute requisite; a gap analysis or SWOT analysis can aid in determining a team's needs. Principal Ben Solly (2013) suggests developing a year-long quality assurance map of processes such as lesson observations and data scrutinies, 'which should all be transparent, with their context and importance understood by all team members'. Head of Humanities Charlotte Ward (2019) concurs; she and her team meet at the beginning, middle and end of the year to evaluate what is going well and why, what could be improved, and the foci for moving forward. When I coordinated English departments, I routinely put development plan review on meeting agendas, which helped us feel assured and in control of outcomes.

Seek out the CPD that you or your team members need; high-performing teams are led by informed middle leaders

If funding is tight, Twitter and Facebook are full of specialty-specific groups that readily share resources and answer questions. I use Twitter to ask for advice about everything from student feedback to how to get out the door in the morning with a feisty toddler. Events like #LeadMeets and #BrewEds are excellent opportunities for networking and perspective-sharing. Ask for a mentor or shadowing opportunity. Do a book study; my colleague and I are working through Mary Myatt's *High Challenge, Low Threat* (2016). Attend a #WomenEd gathering, of course. Access blogs, podcasts, school visits – the list is endless. Accessing CPD outside of traditional school structures has enabled me to lead with insight and certainty.

Innovate, take risks and embrace failure as long as it doesn't hamper learning or morale

Some risks will have fruitful outcomes and others will be flops. My biggest flop is the elective pineapple chart drop-in calendar I introduced to help teachers see each other's lessons. Colleagues expressed support for the philosophy, but ultimately felt like it was 'one more thing'; after spotty participation for a couple of months, it was retired. I believe the mechanism could have been powerful, but it wasn't the right fit for us at the time. My headteacher was supportive and talked me through what didn't work. Not once was I made to feel like a failure. Middle leaders can model this for their teams as well, by 'letting them know it is okay to feel uncomfortable' (Myatt, 2016: 33). Its also important to foster a trusting, collaborative culture, as it is one of the biggest factors in school effectiveness (Kowalski, 2006). I've learned that team health can be bolstered through establishing norms for meetings, ensuring all voices are heard, and saying thank you, which educators don't hear enough. One of my modus operandi has always been to keep things solutions-oriented to stave off negativity, and I know the importance of (sensitively) challenging harmful words and actions. In my school, the middle leaders are exceptional in how they drive progress in their teams whilst nurturing *community*. Our Head of Humanities, for example, organises curry nights open to all, and our Head of Computing and E-learning has devised a whole-school intranet that makes staff *communication* much easier.

SENIOR LEADERS STEER

Entrust your middle leaders, as well as taking responsibility for their performance

If school outcomes are poor, it's easy for senior leaders to point fingers at middle leaders. I saw this at a school where blame was rife, but middle managers were impeded by micromanagement and not offered CPD. We should be reminded that senior leaders 'need to look to ourselves for answers first' (Bendickson, n.d.). My conscientious senior leadership team believes that the trust, support and conditions we do – or don't – put in place for middle leaders are highly influential.

Decentralise!

Sometimes it's tricky handing over the reins when you would do things differently, such as when my Upper School colleague proposed rejigging tutorial programming. In the end, the new, bespoke programme met individual student needs much better and my team felt like they had ownership. Deputy head Erica Warne (2019) says there is a ripple effect of sharing responsibility: 'Empowering others leads to happy teachers and happy students.' I've learned that if a middle leader's initiative has a solid purpose, is well planned and puts no one at a disadvantage, it should be seriously considered.

Provide unequivocal strategic planning and directives

In *Liminal Leadership*, Stephen Tierney writes: 'Part of creating great Middle Leadership and allowing it to flourish is being explicit about what you expect. That is, being explicit to yourself as well as to others' (2016: 34). I try to ensure that my school-wide aims have *clarity*, and that middle leaders know precisely how their work connects with the overall strategic plan. We spend a chunk of time in CPD days at the beginning of the school year defining this.

Support middle leaders in evaluating their work and that of others

I've particularly enjoyed doing this through my colleague's recent National Professional Qualification Senior Leadership programme. She's been facilitating a school-wide literacy project and we meet every few weeks to assess and reflect, a process that's benefitted both of us. On a whole-school level, our senior leadership team asks middle leaders to assess initiatives and policies, as their expertise and knowledge of the pulse of the *community* are imperative.

Establish routines for recognising the good work your middle leaders do

Never, ever take credit for their efforts and actively communicate their accomplishments. Middle leadership, in all its complexity, is a demanding gig, so take every opportunity to bring levity, assurance and celebration in ways that are comfortable to those that you're applauding. As our 'engine room' of the school (Toop, 2013) and the 'heart of the action' (Rogers, 2018), those remarkable people who serve as middle leaders fully deserve it.

Passing on being 10% braver

- Define a vision and ensure it connects with school-wide aims.
- Establish trust, which will make evaluation and oversight easier.
- Take risks - both in innovating and in letting go of preconceived notions.
- Embrace failure as a learning mechanism.

REFERENCES

Bendickson, L. (n.d.) A Dilemma for Senior Leaders: Middle Leadership. Auckland, NZ: The University of Auckland's Centre for Educational Leadership (UACEL). Available at: https://cdn.auckland.ac.nz/assets/education/about/research/starpath/documents/leading-change/resources/A%20Dilemma%20for%20Senior%20Leaders%20-%20Middle%20Leadership.pdf (accessed 10 July 2020).

Berry, J. (2019) 'The power of middle leaders', *jillberry102* blog [Online]. Available at: jillberry102.blog/2019/04/02/the-power-of-middle-leaders/ (accessed 19 August 2019).

Kowalski, T. J. (2006) *The School Superintendent*. London: Sage. Kindle edition.

McKinsey & Co. (2016) *Women in the Workplace 2016* (Report No. 2). [Online]. Available at: https://wiw-report.s3.amazonaws.com/Women_in_the_Workplace_2019_print.pdf (accessed 19 December 2019).

Myatt, M. (2016) *High Challenge, Low Threat*. Woodbridge: John Catt Educational.

Rogers, T. (2018) 'The Secret to Being an Excellent Middle Leader?' *tes*, 16 July [Online]. Available at: www.tes.com/news/secret-being-excellent-middle-leader-master-plan-and-mission-statement (accessed 19 August 2019).

Solly, B. (2013) 'The Seven Secrets to Middle Leadership.' *SecEd: The Voice for Secondary Education*, 14 November [Online]. Available at: www.sec-ed.co.uk/best-practice/the-seven-secrets-to-middle-leadership/ (accessed 1 September 2019).

Tierney, S. (2016) *Liminal Leadership*. Woodbridge: John Catt Educational.

Toop, J. (2013) 'Making the most of middle leaders to drive change in schools.' *The Guardian*, 2 July [Online]. Available at www.theguardian.com/teacher-network/teacher-blog/2013/jul/02/middle-leaders-driving-change-school (accessed 29 July 2020).

Ward, C. (2019) Personal interview, 2 October.

Warne, E. (2019) Personal interview, 26 October.

7

BEING A WOMAN AND A LEADER WITH A DISABILITY

Ruth Golding

KEY POINTS

Being a woman with a physical disability has meant being 10% braver by:

- Accepting my limitations as well as my strengths;
- Tackling the biases and assumptions that are made about disability;
- Asking for my needs to be met in an assertive way;
- Showing high levels of resilience in the face of setbacks.

INTRODUCTION

Kimberlé Crenshaw defined intersectionality as a way of expressing the oppression that African American women experienced in their lives and workplace. The experience of these women was viewed as being twice as oppressive as they faced discrimination because of their gender *and* ethnicity (Crenshaw, 2017). When people have more than one characteristic that provokes discrimination, these multiple characteristics compound negatively, worsening the discrimination. Each part of a person's identity gives them a greater or lesser degree of privilege in society. For example, using an intersectionality calculator (Intersectionality Score Calculator, n.d.) I see that as a white, heterosexual, disabled, well-educated woman, aged over 50, in the UK, 61% of people have more privilege than me, but, conversely, I have more privilege than 39% of the population. For me, lymphoedema in both my legs and right arm has made climbing the career ladder more difficult, sometimes frustrating but not impossible.

The Department for Education (DfE) in England has limited data about disabled educators; 2017 was the last time schools were asked for such data. Only 50% of schools returned the information, which showed only 0.5% identifying as disabled (DfE, 2017). This contrasts with 22% of the working population in the rest of society, according to the Family Resources Survey, 2016/17 (DWP, 2019). There is no data collected by the government on leadership and disability, but when you are working from a starting point of 0.5% this makes women leaders with a disability an incredibly rare group. Several of #WomenEd's core values are helpful in supporting disabled leaders to succeed.

ACCEPT YOUR LIMITATIONS AND RECOGNISE YOUR STRENGTHS: CHANGE

'Yesterday I was clever, so I wanted to *change* the world. Today I am wise, so I am changing myself.' (Rumi, n.d.)

Teaching is a disabling profession, even for an able-bodied person. Images of teachers dragging themselves to the end of the academic year, fuelled by chocolate and crisps, often circulate. Add a disability to this and it can be toxic and cause a disabled person to turn in on themselves and experience self-loathing as they battle with a body that will not do what they want it to. I fought this battle with myself for many years until I embraced my differences and started to love my limitations.

I learned to accept myself by knowing my condition well, taking notice of how my body responded to *change*s in working and sleeping patterns. My condition is painful, and I tire very easily, so I:

- start work very early to enable me to be most effective when I have the most energy, and I have learnt not to feel guilty when I leave before others;
- front-load duties at school to the beginning of the week where I am at my strongest;
- accept being cared for and carry out little or no activity in the evenings and week-ends so that I can rest and recuperate for the working day or week.

The outcome of these *change*s means that I focus on everything that I can do, rather than what I can't do. Being disabled makes you good at inclusion, because you remember that people have needs and you make this central to your practice. You are skilled at developing creative ways to remove barriers and implement reasonable adjustments for both students and colleagues. In addition, a lack of mobility makes you find smart ways of working and use technology for productivity as well as teaching and learning.

Embrace who you are, embrace your limitations and remember that your disability is a blessing as much as a *challenge*. When those moments occur where you feel that it's too hard, believe in yourself. When you do this, you'll be ready and able to rise to the *challenge* of dealing with the assumptions and stereotypes you will face as a disabled woman leader.

TACKLE THE BIASES AND ASSUMPTIONS THAT ARE MADE ABOUT DISABILITY: CHALLENGE

'I hope that we will one day *change* society to fit the unique individual and not the unique individual to fit society.' (Dunham, 2015)

We live at a time when a woman's value is still focused on what we look like, rather than what we do or what we have to offer. The continued objectifying of women in the media means that no one is immune: everyone is socialised into 'attractive equals competent'. A disabled woman leader therefore is disadvantaged on two fronts. Imagine limbs that are distorted, or clothes that don't fit, or the only comfortable shoes you can wear are trainers. Negative assumptions about your ability and professionalism form unconsciously.

When I was younger and very body-conscious, statements like 'You look normal' or 'I have never thought of you as disabled' felt comforting and life-affirming. Next, they made me feel the same as everyone else. As I matured and gained more life experience, I realised that statements like this, no matter how well intentioned, are micro-aggressions that say something negative about how people view disability.

'You look normal' suggests that there are two types of people – us and them. If you are in the 'us' group, you are fine, you're accepted for who you are and your capabilities aren't questioned. If you're in the other group ('them', 'those people'), what is inferred is that you're not one of us, you are different, and therefore there may not be as much investment or belief in you. Watch Vivienne Porritt discuss this on YouTube in 'A world where normal doesn't exist: Celebrating uniqueness' (2018).

'I have never thought of you as disabled' can also seem quite innocuous, even creating *confidence* that your limitations are hidden, and you fit in with your peers. However, behind such a statement is a host of assumptions about disability and what disabled people are like. It turns us into a one-dimensional being, just a disability. We are no longer people with a wide range of skills, talents and attributes. This perspective may seem quite extreme to the non-disabled, but to a disabled woman leader, this needs to be considered and *challenge*d vociferously.

So how can assumptions and biases about disability be *challenge*d?

- Educate people around disability-related biases. Develop learning materials for staff and students that highlight micro-aggressions for disability, gender, race and sexuality.
- Get involved in informal conversations about living with a disability.
- Inform people when the statements they make highlight their biases, and support them to understand the different dimensions of disability.
- Use your leadership position to raise awareness of the skills that disabled people bring to the workplace.
- Ensure your organisation is genuinely positive about disabled people rather than simply displaying 'Positive about Disabled People' symbols in job advertisements. Plan for disability in every aspect of the recruitment process. Does your interview programme have lots of standing, are your materials available in different formats, have you considered people who tire easily, are the resources easy to read, are your instructions straightforward and accessible?

- If you are a leader with disabled people in your organisation, be proactive, find out about them, recognise their skills and talents, view them as an asset, not a problem, and make sure you put in place reasonable adjustments that enable them to do their job well.

HOW TO BE ASSERTIVE AND MAKE YOUR WORKPLACE ACCESSIBLE: COMMUNICATION

'To be passive is to let others decide for you. To be aggressive is to decide for others. To be assertive is to decide for yourself. And to trust that there is enough, that you are enough.' (Edith Eger, 2018: 192)

When you are disabled by a workplace, you must get used to asking people to *change* the way things are done and adjust aspects of your role. They need to view a situation from your perspective and that takes all your negotiation skills. You'd think this would be easy, but for the first half of my teaching career it was something I struggled with. By not making my needs known, I was regularly ill and absent from school which was not good for my students, my colleagues or my career progression! I had to learn to be assertive and communicate that I needed to teach in one room, I couldn't do standing duties, I would need to go home early after late nights and come in later the day after. This all sounds very easy, however don't be fooled: not everyone is receptive to meeting needs. Some people think you are getting special treatment, others resent you, and don't be surprised when you have to remind people of what has been agreed, each and every year. To develop an assertive approach, these suggestions will help:

- Read practical guides to assertiveness such as the classic *A Woman in Your Own Right* by Anne Dickson (2012) or *Dare to Lead* by Brene Brown (2018). Practise the strategies which will make you a better leader and improve your environment. Both books will also build your self-esteem, so that you are a more effective communicator, which is an essential feature of strong leadership.
- Think about what will make your job easier to manage each day, week and term, and map out everything that will improve things and go and ask for it.
- Make a management plan for disability and store it in your personnel file.
- Use line-management meetings to reflect on how reasonable adjustments are working for you and make additional *change*s where necessary.

DEVELOPING A RESILIENT OUTLOOK IN THE FACE OF SETBACKS: CONFIDENCE

'She stood in the storm, and when the wind did not blow her away, she adjusted her sails.' (Elizabeth Edwards, cited in Netter, 2010)

Everyone with a disability knows there will be setbacks over a lifetime. These range from health problems that cause absence from work to being stigmatised or excluded by bad planning. Furthermore, there can be obstacles such as frustratingly slow career progression or no progression at all. Horribly, @DisabilityEdUK hears regularly from disabled people being forced from their roles (although no official statistics exist on this). As disabled leaders, we are the allies for other disabled people and have a responsibility to protect the workforce. It is therefore evident that endless reserves of resilience are required from the disabled leader in order to flourish in these roles.

The first step to resilience is building your *confidence* to lead well:

- Seek and respond to feedback on your plans and projects.
- Get a coach to *challenge* your thinking.
- When the negative voice in your head fills you with self-doubt, silence it.
- Understand that disabled people often experience more ill health than others, so ask for disability-related absences to be recorded separately.
- Continually develop your leadership skills though reading, listening to and learning from others.
- Build a strong and affirming network of leaders who understand equity and diversity.
- Love all that you are and can be; you are enough and you can lead at the highest level.
- If you are disabled and just setting out on your leadership journey, contact @DisabilityEdUK on Twitter for advice and support.
- Be aware of the legislation that prevents discrimination; the Equality and Human Rights Commission is helpful around the law and your rights. The Education Support Network is the charity for UK educators which supports both mental health and wellbeing, and it helped me with a grant for equipment earlier in my career.

Passing on being 10% braver as a disabled woman leader

'The most common way people give up their power is by thinking they don't have any.' (Alice Walker, 2004)

The best advice I can offer is:

- Always remember that you are a strong and capable person; being disabled has made you this way.

(Continued)

- Shining a light on biases diminishes them.
- Being an effective communicator brings people with you and creates communities in common.
- When you love yourself and look after yourself, you will never forget to be yourself.

REFERENCES

Brown, B. (2018) *Dare to Lead*. London: Vermilion.

Crenshaw, K. (2017) 'Intersectionality, more than two decades later', *Columbia Law School*, 8 June [Online]. Available at: www.law.columbia.edu/pt-br/news/2017/06/kimberle-crenshaw-intersectionality (accessed 28 August 2019).

Department for Education (DfE) (2017) School Workforce in England 2016 [Online]. Available at: https://assets.publishing.service.gov.uk/government/uploads/system/uploads/attachment_data/file/620825/SFR25_2017_MainText.pdf#page8 (accessed 30 September 2019).

Department for Work and Pensions (DWP) (2019) Family Resources Survey 2016/17, 28 March [Online]. Available at: https://assets.publishing.service.gov.uk/government/uploads/system/uploads/attachment_data/file/692771/family-resources-survey-2016-17.pdf (accessed 3 January 2020).

Dickson, A. (2012) *A Woman in Your Own Right: Assertiveness and You*. London: Quartet.

Dunham, L. (2015) 'Lena Dunham interviews Gloria Steinem', *Harper's Bazaar*, 19 November [Online]. Available at: www.harpersbazaar.com/culture/features/a12838/lena-dunham-gloria-steinem-interview-1215 (accessed 30 September 2019).

Eger, E. (2018) *The Choice*. London: Rider.

Intersectionality Score Calculator (n.d.) Homepage [Online]. Available at: https://intersectionalityscore.com (accessed 28 August 2019).

Netter, S. (2010) 'Elizabeth Edwards: In her own words', *ABC News*, 7 December [Online]. Available at: www.abcnews.go.com/US/elizabeth-edwards-words/story?id=12337723. (accessed 3 January 2020).

Porritt, V. (2018) 'A world where normal doesn't exist: Celebrating uniqueness', *YouTube*, 16 July [Online]. Available at: https://youtu.be/YVbtBtw9Th0 (accessed 3 January 2020).

Rumi (n.d.) Rumi - Quotable Quotes. Available at: www.goodreads.com/quotes/551027-yesterday-i-was-clever-so-i-wanted-to-*change*-the (accessed 25 January 2020).

Walker, A. (2004) As quoted in *The Best Liberal Quotes Ever : Why the Left is Right* by William P. Martin, p. 173. Illinois: Sourcebooks, Inc.

8

INVESTING IN OURSELVES AS LEADERS: A GUILTY PLEASURE?

Lacey Austin and Kerry Jordan-Daus

KEY POINTS

This chapter will:

- Advocate that making time for ourselves is important for our professional development as leaders in education and our future leadership roles;
- Show how we need to *challenge* widely held views that our time should be spent on work and family and not on ourselves;
- Explain that we want to lead by example, showing others that it is not an act of selfishness to put ourselves first.

INTRODUCTION

Currently, we are in the final stage of our professional doctorate in education (EdD): Lacey, assistant headteacher and mother of two young daughters, and Kerry, senior leader at a university and mother of a young adult with special educational needs (SEN). This is the story of conversations we have had over the course of our study. We would like to share with you how we have made sense of the competing dynamics encountered whilst following an academic programme of study as part of our professional development, or, put another way, all those little voices in our heads telling us that we are being selfish. This is our story of sense making during our study and of the costs and *challenge*s of investing in our professional development. We tell our story as to why this is important for all women, to encourage others to see their professional development as important in smashing that glass ceiling and being role models for our colleagues and for our daughters.

TAKING TIME: INVESTING IN SELF, PROFESSIONAL AND PERSONAL EMPOWERMENT

We met on our education doctorate programme (EdD) and, over the course of the last three years, we have had many discussions about time, self, professional lives and family. In discussing our decision and determination to make space and take time out of busy lives to complete an EdD, we believe that we have been 10% braver (Cowley, 2019). We have refused to be silenced by guilt or toxic shame for spending time on developing our careers and investing in ourselves and our future. Yet, as women, carving out this time can feel more like an expense than an asset (Schulte, 2019). By an expense, we mean a luxury, taking us away from our seemingly traditional duties or responsibilities. By a luxury, we mean, why would you choose to go to the library all day Saturday to write a doctoral essay instead of visiting elderly parents or doing the cleaning?

Lacey

Why, as women, do we see time for professional development as a luxury? Why do we so often feel that we are not worthy of it or need to ask permission for it? I have been working on my doctorate whilst working as an assistant headteacher. I had one child. I took a short interruption when I had a second child. Returning to study was a big commitment but not a luxury item; it's not like a new pair of shoes, but, yes, I knew it would require time to myself. I did discuss the time and financial commitment with my husband; it had to be a team effort. It doesn't stop it being a bone of contention at times, especially during busy periods in the school year. I knew I wasn't going to have lots of time for myself; I knew it was going to take up a lot of my weekends and evenings, and involve making lots of sacrifices.

Kerry

I had already started studying for a doctorate twice before. This is third time lucky. I gave up before because of work, new roles and promotions and family commitments. I couldn't or didn't find the time. Juggling having a senior leadership role at the university and being the primary carer for a young adult with learning disabilities, there was never enough time for me. But perhaps I am more selfish now, or, rather, I am putting myself first?

Schulte (2019) describes how 'women's time has been interrupted and fragmented throughout history' and reminds us that 'concentrated time you can control is something women have never had the luxury to expect, at least not without getting slammed for unseemly selfishness'.

Lacey

Until I started the EdD, I consumed myself with work: eat, sleep, work. The EdD enabled me to step out of that and look at what I was doing through different lenses, and now I have a healthier relationship with work, school and my leadership. I even recognised that I needed a more flexible arrangement at school without sacrificing my leadership role.

Kerry

I didn't tell my family for some time that I had started again. It was my secret; perhaps my guilty secret. I am not sure why I kept it a secret. I was really working hard and maybe I thought I was asking too much of others to support me in giving even more time. Maybe I also felt selfish? There was always more work to do, or more I could do to support my daughter. Not having the doctorate has been detrimental to my career in higher education. So, I guess, yes, I have hit my glass ceiling.

This phenomenon of seeing investment in ourselves as a luxury has been highlighted by Rogers (2017) as a factor in understanding the glass ceiling, drawing particular attention to how a lack of time to invest in ourselves and the guilt of it 'paralyses' women climbing up the career ladder (Gill and Donaghue, 2016: 96).

Kerry

Of course, our partners are perfectly capable of looking after children and doing the shopping, but that isn't the issue, is it? It's what is in our head, or what society expects, or what we think society expects. I read on Twitter a male leader in education discussing his sacrifice when asked how he found the time to study for his EdD. Interestingly, he didn't mention anything about family commitments. It's not just kids; it's now, for me, looking after elderly parents too and the shame of not doing that carer stuff. I took my books on our Christmas holiday in Norfolk and sat at the kitchen table when the family had gone to bed, writing my assignment.

Lacey

I am not going to lie, I have certainly spent many hours navigating the twilight zone (Gibson et al., 2017), reading and writing late into the night. That's where I found the time.

Many a Saturday I will hide myself away in the university library whilst the girls go to football with their dad and grandparents. I am always told how lucky I am; does this make it a luxury? I am not sure that a man gets the same questioning about a decision to invest in his professional development. As a mum of two young children, yes, there have been a few who have raised an eyebrow and looked at me in a way that I have interpreted as disapproval.

But being part of the #WomenEd *community* has given me the *confidence* to successfully negotiate with my school, with my family, with my friends and with myself. Just to say though, this is not a luxury, this is about me and my professional development.

Through our doctoral group, we have provided encouragement, support and *challenge*; not formalised peer mentoring or coaching, but, on review, something that might fit a definition of effective peer coaching, a non-hierarchical and 'highly accepting, lets-work-on-what-matters-at-the-moment relationship' (Clutterbuck, 2009: 103, in

Kram and Isabella, 1985) and the 'mutuality that enables both individuals to experience being the giver and the receiver' (Kram and Isabella, 1985: 118). We would both argue that peer coaching can be a powerful and empowering tool to support the advancement of professional lives (Clutterbuck, 2009, in Dram and Isabella, 1985; Lofthouse, 2015).

Lacey

Talking about all this has enabled me to be at peace, but it has taken a long time. For the first two years, I felt fear, shame and guilt. Have I overstretched myself? What about the potential embarrassment if I step down? Statistically, working-class women from my kind of background don't do doctorates. July 2018 was the breakthrough moment: an essay I wrote enabled me to carve out some personal space or what I now think of as my third space, 'a dynamic space in between work and home' (Gibson et al., 2017: 173).

Kerry

I absolutely loved that essay; I wrote it at a time of huge work-related upheaval. I recall the tutor saying to me that she didn't know how I found the mental strength to write. Writing the essay gave me a mental strength and this made me more resilient within a challenging work environment. I stayed strong during a period of *change* and the EdD gave me a theoretical framework to see what was happening. It was also my third space.

Lacey

I am very different in my leadership role now. I like to think I have wider perspective and a critical voice and, equally importantly, I have achieved a healthier work–life balance. I have embraced my identity and its multiple facets. I feel a responsibility to role-model for my daughters and that outweighs any guilt or toxic shame. The ultimate goal of being successful for me is that my daughters will not define this space as a luxury but as their given right which they will never question.

Kerry

I can see that I am a stronger leader now. These are times of huge *change*s in universities. My studying has in fact helped me be in a better place and my mental health has improved. I do feel much more in control of my destiny, who I am and what I can be. That's interesting because we started talking about feelings of guilt at the time being devoted to study and now we are both saying that we are in better places professionally and personally. Looking back over our conversation, I can see how this has empowered us, our children and no doubt others with whom we work. It disrupts the discourse about what women can do. We both talked about our identity and aligned with our gender and the expectations upon us; I do feel stronger, and that is healthier in every sense. This isn't a privileged place for the few, but something I believe is within the grasp of so many more women.

Passing on being 10% braver

- *Confidence:* there's never a better time, a good time, the right time - start your Masters or doctorate now, or join us at a #WomenEd event.

- *Community:* build your network of co-learners whilst studying.

- *Collaboration:* give support to others and lean on others for help - embrace the mutuality of support though peer coaching.

- *Clarity:* identify your time and protect it: negotiate with your family and employer for some protected time for professional development - if you don't ask you don't get.

- *Communication:* watch your language; don't apologise for investing in yourself - don't let it be seen as a guilty pleasure.

REFERENCES

Cowley, S. (2019) '10% Braver: Feel the fear and do it anyway', in V. Porritt and K. Featherstone (eds), *10% Braver: Inspiring Women to Lead in Education*. London: Sage, pp. 15–24.

Gibson, P., Shanks, R. and Dick, S. (2017) 'The EdD and one bedtime story more! An exploration of the Third-Space inhabited by mothers working in educational leadership whilst studying for a professional doctorate', *Management in Education, 31*(4): 172–9.

Gill, R. and Donaghue, N. (2016) 'Resilience, apps and reluctant individualism: Technologies of self in neoliberal academy', *Women's Studies International Forum, 54*: 91–9.

Kram, K. E. and Isabella, L. A. (1985) 'Mentoring alternatives: The role of peer relationships in career development', *Academy of Management Journal, 28*(1): 108–36.

Lofthouse, R. (2015) 'Beyond mentoring; peer coaching by and for teachers. Can it live up to its promise?', *BERA blog*, 15 May. Available at: www.bera.ac.uk/blog/beyond-mentoring-peer-coaching-by-and-for-teachers-can-it-live-up-to-its-promise (accessed 23 October 2019).

Rogers, C. (2017) '"I'm complicit and I'm ambivalent and that's crazy": Care-less spaces for women in the academy', *Women's Studies International Forum, 61*: 115–22.

Schulte, B. (2019) 'A woman's greatest enemy? A lack of time to herself', *The Guardian*, 21 July. Available at: www.theguardian.com/commentisfree/2019/jul/21/woman-greatest-enemy-lack-of-time-themselves (accessed 15 August 2019).

PART 2
ADVOCATING FOR OTHERS

9
STAND BY YOUR WOMAN
Andy Mitchell

KEY POINTS

This chapter will:

- Explain why I needed to be 10% braver for my partner;
- Explain how I try to support my partner when she is being 10% braver;
- Try not to assume everyone has an identical relationship to us!

INTRODUCTION

Whilst working in a special school, I was in a meeting and one of the professionals outlined what staff and school were doing for a particular student. Essentially, they were clearing everything out of the way so that the student could concentrate fully on their studies. The professional added that the student was now able to work to their maximum capacity and could only do that because of the endeavours by staff around the student. The analogy she used was that it is like someone travelling through a dense jungle but having people around them to clear the bush so they can make progress. When I was asked to write this chapter, it was one of the first things I thought of.

Quite simply, I can't do the things my wife does. She runs a school. She is a founding member and strategic leader of #WomenEd. She is part of the Headteachers' Round-table. She writes regular articles and blogs and genuinely helps anyone who needs it. She's even co-editing this book.

Of course, not every woman leader will be a headteacher and yet the demand remains the same. Over the years, we have adjusted the way we interact and work together to adapt to each of our life *change*s and career *change*s. When we met, I worked in business; I took a substantial pay cut to work in a school when she became pregnant because I wanted the same holidays as my wife and child. Not everyone will want to do this. However, at each point in time that there was a *change*, we have consciously articulated what any possible issues might be. Usually, it's her feeling terrific guilt about having less time with us, being grumpier or needing to sleep more. Do I want my wife to be happy? Yes. Does this mean we have to be flexible? Absolutely.

OUR HOME

What I can do is help to clear everything out of the way on occasion so my wife can focus on what she needs to do. Obviously, I can't do this all the time and it is an unspoken reciprocal arrangement we have. I work full time but I make sure the jobs I take allow me to help with childcare and running the family as a team. I have recently taken a job closer to our daughter's school to help with that. Our pre-teen is struggling to get up in the morning, which is making my wife late for school. As a headteacher, you don't want to turn up late after an argument and battle to wake your daughter; this is something that I've therefore taken on.

We have a cleaner, which really helps (there are now far fewer arguments about dusting and a calm environment to return to on a Friday evening); I'm the one to make sure we have food in the house and I cook most nights. Left to my partner, she'd just snack on crackers or order takeaway. I take care of the washing and ironing over the weekend purely so my wife can sleep and recharge her batteries, ready for the next exhausting week.

This may sound as if I've slipped neatly into a reversed traditional 1950s housewife role – this is not the case. It is certainly not the sort of home life either myself or my partner experienced growing up – mums did the housework, and we have tried hard to share out the load equally. We've looked at our strengths and what we enjoy and have attempted to split things between us. She organises the holidays, the pets, remembers cards and presents; she is completely supportive of my own further studies and ensures I have the space and time to complete this. Given my choice, we'd never *change* a duvet cover and all the walls would be painted in Brighton & Hove Albion colours. It makes for a more harmonious home.

OUR FAMILY

What I can do for her is also do all I can to ensure that our family is a relatively happy and healthy one. Raising just one daughter together may not seem that tricky to those with lots of kids – but we have struggled. Only by working as a partnership have we been able to make it work. Keziah's family is in Somerset and mine is in Sussex, while we live in the Midlands. We were not expecting to become parents but our daughter was a little miracle and her stubbornness in the womb was nothing compared to her stubbornness now. Even experienced birth, foster and adoptive parents conclude she is 'hard work'. But we love her most.

Keziah was an assistant headteacher when our daughter was born. She had taken maternity leave for less than a week when she was born and returned to school four months later. I know she took a lot of flack for this from colleagues, mostly other women, who whispered behind her back and made comments about her re-evaluating her priorities. All I could do was support her and listen. Wading in and fighting her battles was not going to help and I'm not her knight in shining armour. Given how frustrated she was by these comments, I am not surprised at all that she went on to co-found #WomenEd – she always said something had to *change* to make such decisions normal.

Being parents is a partnership and it helps if you both leave any stereotypes at the door of the midwife. Managing a career whilst being a parent is hard work but society puts much more pressure on mothers. All any partner can do is ensure they take an equal share of the responsibility when they can, even if it's not the same all day every day.

Luckily, we did not get many comments from our parents. We live very different lives to the ones they lived but neither have been judgemental about the choices we have made. They are far more likely to be critical about the acquisition of a new dog than anything family and work related. I know we're quite lucky in that respect because I am aware of how many people have to endure helpful comments from visiting in-laws.

Our family is always quite busy. Keziah works a lot and, even when not focused on her main headteacher job, she is absorbed by #WomenEd, the Headteachers' Roundtable, edutwitter, politics and supporting those she knows. It is hardly a strain to look after our daughter when she goes off to a conference, although for the last two #WomenEd unconferences she has gone with her mum. We are open about what we enjoy doing and we try to squeeze as much of this into our time as possible, planning for it to happen rather than hoping it will: visiting family and friends, travelling abroad, going to the cinema, eating in our favourite restaurants. Every weekend we plan to do something, and we make sure it happens – even if that means going out in storms or snow. Personally, I'd rather watch the football, *Top Gear* or *Homes Under the Hammer*, but, for the sake of all of our sanities, we do things as a family.

I think that when we were children, and neither of us grew up in an affluent home, family was just something that you were an unthinking part of. Now we work really hard, and consciously so, at making it a possible safe space for us all.

OUR DIFFICULTIES

What I can also do is be a source of support and motivation. Even though my wife knows what she is doing and where she is going, she still has doubts and fears. Being able to listen and offer some advice, I hope, helps – or at least she says it does – by offering the support and reassurance that her plans are right, even if I am completely unqualified and under-experienced to do so. I often have absolutely no idea what she is talking about, but I can still be available.

Being there when things go wrong, to help with the pathway forward, is complete and utter support, even when things look bleak. Twice she has been in jobs where her boss was an unreasonable bully who made her life and work a misery. There was very little I could do, except to listen and reassure her when she knew she had to look elsewhere for a new job. It's incredibly frustrating when all I could do was reassure her that the bullies were the problem and not her; that if she wanted to take a step backwards, we'd happily downsize and start again somewhere else. It is about constantly reminding her that we will do whatever it takes and she is not alone. Frankly, she earns more money than I do, and I know she feels the responsibility of being the main breadwinner. There is no point us shifting traditional gender roles if all that happens is women end up with the same stresses as traditional male breadwinners. Therefore, I have never seen it as my role to tell her either to stay in a job or to leave a job; her career is hers and I am just a sounding board.

Pretty much everyone working in education, male or female, leader or not, will have a bad time. It was the same when I worked in business. Keziah doesn't often unload on me – she often can't because of confidentiality or safeguarding – but I know to look for the tells and when I notice them (and I can be a bit slow at this) I simply adjust around her – it might be choosing to watch her programmes on TV, or suggesting doing something I wouldn't normally want to do. Regardless of your partner's role, we all need to pay attention to sometimes imperceptible mood shifts – even if that does seem impossible!

It's fair to say that there are times when, despite thinking I've done everything possible to help and support, it's still not enough. It's hard to see it when close up but the enormity of what she does is staggering. Sometimes I think I'm kidding myself that what I do goes any way to help the situation. And, from time to time, it does all get too much, but this is probably true of any job or relationship. As well as the usual difficult decisions any headteacher must make, she insists on working in challenging schools in areas of deprivation – so there are many additional hardships she sees and experiences every day.

In addition, she has been personally targeted by various people – not just on social media, but in real life too, and this would eat away at anyone. It exhausts her and makes her question what she is doing. Working in a toxic environment, being targeted on social media, receiving malicious *communications* or your professionalism being questioned, are not things unique to female headteachers – it can happen to anyone at any time.

No matter what I say, what I do or how I try to help, it isn't always enough. All I can do is be there because I know she is there for me too.

Passing on being 10% braver

- Do what is right for your family and don't let anyone else's expectations influence you.

- Think: What can I do to make my partner's life a bit easier?

- Make sure you communicate effectively so that supporting each other is completely honest and reciprocal.

- Something will go wrong at some time - it has to be accepted - so work these things out together without blaming anyone.

10
STAND BY ALL WOMEN

Keziah Featherstone with Jon Chaloner, Vic Goddard,
Dan Morrow and Malcolm Richards

KEY POINTS

This chapter will:

- Explain why #WomenEd has been 10% braver by actively advocating for #HeForShe voices within the movement;
- Encourage men to be 10% braver by supporting what can sometimes be seen as a female-only crusade;
- Enable different male perspectives on female leadership to be heard so that others may learn from their mistakes and succeed.

INTRODUCTION

Why do we need men? Why does feminism or #WomenEd need male allies? Isn't #HeForShe just a little bit patronising and sexist?

Since #WomenEd's inception, we have always been clear that this is a not a separatist movement. When we are serving a *community* of young people who are of all genders, it would be at odds to celebrate one gender more than the other(s). Women want to work alongside men as respected equals, as professionals and as advocates for a more diverse world. To write off approximately half the population seems churlish.

Indeed, the established patriarchy will only be effectively dismantled when those from within make a conscious decision to be part of the team dismantling it – either through coaxing or by way of dynamite. Simply put, any revolution needs allies if it is to succeed, not because one voice is more authoritative or valid than another's but because all voices amplifying the message makes it very loud and clear: this has to *change* and *change* now.

HOW TO BE A GOOD MALE ALLY TO WOMEN LEADERS

Dan Morrow – CEO of Dartmoor Multi Academy Trust

The emergence of #HeForShe in 2014 crystallised the call for men who wanted to reject a narrative of toxic masculinity and promote an increasingly diverse political and social reality. There is no doubt that the concept of 'male ally' has gained increasing traction, so what does it mean each and every day?

Male allies are men who associate with, cooperate with and support women. However, this basic definition does not begin to describe the complexities inherent in the term. There is a potential tension between attitudes, which may well be supportive and cooperative, with behaviours which may not always accord. In essence, being an ally is an act, not a position.

The first important strand of being a good ally is to understand and accept that the issue of women's leadership is my responsibility. It is the responsibility of all within the system, but most especially for those who are the traditional and historic holders of power. By actively choosing to yield (not give) power, we signal *change*. We help others to become the *change* by initially changing ourselves. Ensuring that male colleagues are advocates is the key foundation here. Men must become aware of their own bias and see through a true lens the dominant system in most organisations of (white) male culture; and that this culture affects and shapes the behaviour of all employees, not merely the leaders.

One of the strongest acts of being a good male ally is in the private advocacy for equity, inclusion and diversity. We must help female colleagues to overcome the conditioning of a patriarchal system that introduces questions of *confidence* and efficacy that many men do not encounter in the same way. This can be supported through public acts, such as policy *change*s within the trust, brokering coaching and leadership development support or through formalised leadership pathways. Essentially, the aim is the same: ensuring that women leaders have the space, capacity, *confidence* and support to explore their own agency and to then define, in their own language and planning, what that will then look like in practice.

The second important strand of being a good ally to women leaders is to be relentless in focus. There is a significant and well-explored intention gap between the efforts of the last 20 years to focus on and drive gender equality with the actual results. Inequality remains stubbornly persistent for women at all levels, in most professions. *Change*s to rules, policies and practice are clearly important in adapting the legally enforceable structures for allegiance and support. However, without a strong culture of advocacy from male leaders, the unwritten rules of the way that power is actually wielded in reality will not alter. Here, male leaders must understand the cultural importance of publically signalling support, advocacy and sponsorship for women leaders, in order to see a true shift in the cultural dynamic within an institution and indeed society at large.

Once the private support and the public message have started to embed, then the final phase of a structural approach to being a good male ally is to ensure that the culture evolves to one where the leadership of women is no longer an exception, but is the expectation. Women as leaders, especially senior leaders and headteachers, must become 'the way we do things around here' and be so usualised that it is only those who are external to the organisation that comment on it. This culture then becomes not just valued but also precious to the people who are part of it; a culture of which we can be proud.

Overall, I believe a good male ally must be *acting* in a way to reduce and then eliminate gender inequalities; through genuinely understanding and valuing diversity and searching for equity rather than mere equality.

BUT YOU ARE A MAN!

Malcolm Richards, teacher, researcher and activist – with Aya, Neneh and Charlie Richards

Schools are spaces with high levels of female representation. For example, in roles across our primary school *community*, at least 74% of full-time teachers and 77% of headteachers are women (DfE, 2018: 32). I have been privileged to work with many inspiring and successful women. I have learnt from observing their practice and under their mentorship, and, as my career has progressed, I have in turn helped develop female leaders. I hope that they would say that I have strived to create professional spaces which are open, safe and progressive for everyone, regardless of gender.

As a black male, I am conscious of both the privileges afforded to me as a man, whilst also experiencing the frustrations of navigating a system that is structurally racist. According to the Department of Education, less than 7% of all state school headteachers are from an 'ethnic minority' (2018: 34) and less than 4% are women (DfE, 2020). Our institutions are designed to uphold the colonial and colonising versions of gender and race which are embodied in the structures, practices and knowledge we are all expected to (without question) 'teach'.

My experience suggests that to be a good ally, you should:

- Recognise your privilege and keep it in check;
- Where you can, use your agency to create spaces where female voices are amplified;

- Foster *confidence* and self-belief;
- Recognise the different needs of your co-workers;
- Create a flexible and supportive work environment;
- Be humble and work to *change* your behaviour.

However, this conversation with my wife and daughters reminds me of the importance of authenticity and honesty in advice giving and reflection:

Daughter 1	(peering over my shoulder): What are you writing?
Me:	I've been asked to write about being a good ally to women.
Daughter 1:	Cool!
Wife:	Why did they ask you?
Me:	I guess because I am a school leader, and have been an advocate for women in my career?
Wife:	[side-eye]
Daughter 2:	Dad, you've got to write about women?
Me:	Yep, about supporting women leaders.
Daughter 2:	But you are a man!
Wife:	… and you aren't always a good ally when it comes to helping at home.
Daughters 1 and 2 with serious faces:	Yeah, tell the truth, Dad.
Me:	[shame]

The truth is that there will have been many other times when I have been aware of behaviour, whether mine or someone else's, either consciously or unconsciously, and not *challenge*d it in the ways I should have.

I believe many of the women I have worked with will say that I am collaborative and have helped create spaces where we can all speak and be heard. Others will acknowledge that I credit origins, authorship and ownership.

I try to *challenge* gender inequality when I see it. I promote women leaders by amplifying their voices and offering the space and place for their expression.

Am I a good ally to women leaders?

NOW WE KNOW WHAT IT (TRULY) FEELS LIKE TO BE THE 'ODD ONE OUT'

Jon Chaloner, CEO of GLF Schools; and Vic Goddard, CEO of PCLC

Without hesitation, we both agreed to attend the second #WomenEd unconference. Why wouldn't we? After all, we have been to lots of education leadership events and we'd only been asked to do a 'panel' session at the unconference. Supporting #WomenEd was not something that took much thinking about. As CEOs, we are responsible for the employment of thousands of people (mainly Jon rather than Vic, of course!), with the majority being women; it was important we took the opportunity to gain a new perspective.

So why on earth were we both so nervous on the way to the #WomenEd event? Was it because it was #WomenEd and we are men? Would we be welcome? Or, rather, what would our welcome look like? For the first time in our professional lives, we were attending an event where the vast majority of people attending didn't look the same as us; where almost all the speakers didn't look like us either! We were suddenly wracked with self-doubt. Asking ourselves whether we should be here? Questioning whether using the word 'ladies' was acceptable in the phrase 'ladies and gentlemen', or should it be 'women and gentlemen'? Despite always trying to be thoughtful in the language we use, we were both suffering with self-doubt and fairly scared to open our mouths for fear of saying something 'incorrect' or drawing attention to ourselves for the wrong reasons.

It suddenly felt uncomfortable being a man attending a conference … it suddenly felt like being a woman going to almost every education leadership conference for the last 20+ years!

It is undeniable how much we learned that day just by being there and having the feelings that we had. We left with no doubt that we'd both benefitted from a system that was set up to be accessible to us and to make us feel comfortable, whilst doing the opposite to many of the other attendees. However, our most significant learning was that it was acceptable to not have all the answers and to ask questions, rather than being scared to open our mouths.

At #WomenEd, we did not encounter any evidence of negativity towards men in leadership roles; just a desire for equality of opportunity. One question to the panel asked how male leaders can help to make *change*. This is indeed the *challenge*. We remain staunchly #HeForShe and, before we are accused of being painfully 'woke', that isn't because it is the latest bandwagon, it is because we are committed to doing the best for our school communities and, by default yet consciously, our wider society.

We are fully focused on developing environments that are the best for the young people and staff we serve – all of them. As school leaders, we have both seen the huge benefit of creating teams that are representative and balanced from a gender perspective. Let's be honest, it is easy to develop an environment that never *challenges* the status quo (our own status quo, of course), but if we do that we miss out on the vast number of possibilities for new thinking and therefore new solutions. To ensure our commitment to #HeForShe, together we must build a responsive system that enables talented women to remain in education, and that allows them to flourish as leaders. We both know that we don't always get things right but it has been great to feel able to ask questions, knowing we will get answers, not judgement.

We accept that we have not always got things right and won't always do so in the future. We hear the little voice in our heads joining in with 'but where is International Men's Day?' exclamations, but now we have the experience of our first unconference to stop and to think differently – although it doesn't *yet* come completely naturally all the time. Now we have an answer to our little voice and, in that particular example, it shouts back 'every day'!

Passing on being 10% braver to male allies

- Openly embrace the values of #WomenEd, even if you're worried about making mistakes and saying the wrong thing.
- Actively look for ways to *challenge* unconscious (and conscious) bias in the workplace.
- Use your privilege to establish and maintain family-friendly schools for all: this will only aid in the recruitment and retention of high-quality staff.

REFERENCES

Department for Education (DfE) (2018) School Leadership in England 2010 to 2016: Characteristics and Trends [Online]. Available at: https://assets.publishing.service.gov.uk/government/uploads/system/uploads/attachment_data/file/725118/Leadership_Analysis_2018.pdf (accessed 12 April 2020).

Department for Education (DfE) (2020) School Teacher Workforce: By Gender and Ethnicity (Headteachers only) [Online]. Available at: www.ethnicity-facts-figures. service.gov.uk/workforce-and-business/workforce-diversity/school-teacher-workforce/ latest#by-ethnicity-and-gender-headteachers-only (accessed 12 April 2020).

11

IF THERE ISN'T A SEAT AROUND THE TABLE, BE THE ONE WHO BUYS THE CHAIRS

Hilary Goldsmith

KEY POINTS

This chapter will:

- Explore my battle for the school business leadership *community* to be taken seriously as school leaders;
- Tell the story of how I used social media to be 10% braver and found my voice;
- Explain why I had to be braver still to seek the support of all women education leaders to embrace school business professionals as peers.

INTRODUCTION

We've seen the figures for the gender balance in teaching. The data shared by The Future Leaders Trust that led to the birth of #WomenEd show that although 85% of primary teachers are female, 71% of primary heads are women. At secondary, with 64% female teachers, only 36% make it into headship (2015). It's clearly tough for a female teacher to achieve a senior leadership role. Imposter syndrome, lack of self-belief, patriarchy, social conditioning? Some or all of these may be the cause, and moving into a senior leadership position can certainly be a daunting prospect for any female educator. It was for me.

Imagine then being an aspiring female leader of education who carries the burden of not having a teaching qualification! That's like turning up for a job as the boss of a lumberjack company without owning an axe or a checked shirt! I mean, why even bother, right? Right. Welcome to the world of the female school business leader (SBL), the most fish-out-of-water job in education. SBLs have it all going on; we don't have battles to contend with, we're fighting a full-out thermo-nuclear war!

THE WORKING MUM STEREOTYPE

First, the profession is dominated by women. Although no formal data exists, we can extrapolate from the ISBL School Business Professional Workforce Survey Report (2020: 8) that approximately 87% of SBLs are female. The stereotype of mums working in the office creates a significant barrier for female SBLs to be taken seriously. Many in education and beyond view the SBL role as a glorified secretary, arranging domestics for the (probably male) headteacher's day. We fight to be seen as qualified, valid professionals. Most SBLs can recount multiple occasions where their role has been interpreted by others as administrative for the teaching professionals who are running a school. Imagine living the cliché of being one of 'the girls in the office', as you fight to promote yourself as a strategic, financial, business expert with every right to sit around your school's senior leadership table. For many SBLs, this remains a significant barrier.

Next, many SBLs are term time only, so aren't considered serious professionals. That doesn't mean they don't work as hard as other school leaders, just that they don't get paid for 13/52nds of it. Many are working parents, so family commitments float around us like wet pyjamas in the bronze swimming award of life. We're clearly not rocking up at the equality party any time soon. Ours is still a profession which is delivered by women but led by men. A large proportion of SBLs have worked their way up from junior administrative roles to financial and business leadership positions, and are people who, despite the hard graft of this demanding and specialist role, struggle to be taken seriously in senior positions. I hear of many SBLs, members of school senior leadership teams, who are expected to make tea, order biscuits and take notes, which leads us to the biggest battle of all.

BEING DEFINED BY WHAT YOU ARE NOT

We are not teachers. And this remains the biggest hurdle. However forward-thinking and liberal the teaching profession thinks it is, there are herds of dinosaurs roaming the educational landscape who refuse to take heed of any individual without Qualified Teacher Status. These Mesozoic doormen refuse entry to their serious educator club to any wannabe who doesn't hold a teacher membership card. It's a bit like Equity, but without the tap dancing. Some schools use the term 'non-teachers' to describe professionals operating in schools who aren't teachers. Imagine how it feels to be identified by the thing that you're not. That's what has bothered me the most since I started working in education in the early 2000s.

THE POWER OF TWITTER

But then there was Twitter, and, on Twitter, everyone has an equal voice and a chance to join the conversation. I started a social media feed for our school goats (@varndeangoats), which attracted the attention of influential people. It seemed I had a talent for being cheeky, irreverent and downright rude, and it's easy to be outspoken and sassy when you're pretending to be a herd of pygmy goats. It's a bit harder when it's you, putting yourself out there in your anxious, socially awkward, imposter-syndromic oddness. But writing is a powerful force, and once I started, I couldn't stop. So, I wrote. I blogged, tweeted and posted and found that the more I wrote, the more I had to say. And the more I was heard.

When you're employed by a school in a senior position, it's difficult to find a balance whereby you can blog and write freely about education policy, and be outspoken about the impact of funding cuts on our schools and the pressures of school leadership, without risking painting your own school in a bad light (and being sacked). But I believe that *change* will only be effected when real practitioners are brave enough to speak up and work together to offer solutions. I did, I do and I will continue to use my voice to ensure that my profession is heard (I haven't been sacked yet).

MY SHERO

And it wasn't only other SBLs who were interested in what I had to say. With the encouragement of the glorious Ann Mroz (editor and digital publishing director of *tes*), I wrote regular blogs and articles for *tes* and other educational publications. Ann is something of a heroine to me; a hugely successful, hard-working woman who inspires me by championing the causes and voices that make our world a better place. I would describe her as my fairy godmother, but even 10% braver isn't brave enough to deal with the unholy mess of gender stereotypical carnage that image invokes in a #WomenEd book. Let's go with shero instead.

MAPPING AN ONLINE COMMUNITY

A small group of school business leaders came together on Twitter to form a *community*. We created SBL-specific hashtags and, by following and retweeting each other's posts, a supportive and welcoming culture. As SBLs, our traditional position is in the back office, but on social media, school business leaders began to speak directly about life in educational business management. There is much wrong with our English education system at present and SBLs were 10% braver in raising their concerns through examples of the impact of funding cuts, the state of school infrastructure and forced cuts to administration and pastoral support services.

And, as more SBL voices were heard, it became easier for others to speak. A *community* emerged that was supportive and collaborative, with the desire to encourage others to join and be a part of the wider educational debate. Conversations started and *connections* were made. I created a Google map where SBLs could plot their location and we watched the *community* grow. It also enabled people to connect with each other in person and to feel part of something bigger. Being an SBL can be a lonely and isolated job, and it's tough to know where to go to get support. An online *community* was the perfect solution. Some of us volunteered as Twitter buddies to support new members to start with social media. We created online resources for new Twitter users and added new SBLs to my 'SBLs on Twitter' list, to encourage our *community* to follow and support each other.

SUPPORTING THE SUPPORT STAFF

As a profession, I know many school business leaders are natural introverts who feel comfortable in the role of quiet and efficient organiser rather than strident leader, and many leave public speaking and assertiveness to others. I know that because I am that. I also know that comfort zones aren't the places to go if you want to develop as a leader, which is why I push myself to take part in wider debates about education. If we want to be credible leaders, we need to model and embody such behaviour. The worst that can happen is that we are ignored, which leaves us no worse off than when we started. So why on earth wouldn't you give it a go? It might just make a difference.

FINDING A FRIENDLY TABLE

But the real *challenge* in being 10% braver was to get a seat around the bigger table where the policy makers and system leaders sit. And that table is in a restaurant that usually has Qualified Teacher Status as an entry requirement. One of the great things about being a school business leader is that you know a lot about tables, and chairs, and you can get a pretty good discount on either. So instead of waiting to be offered a seat, I dug deep into my bravery bank account, found the cash to buy my own chair, plonked it down at the edge of the table, and, instead of being asked to leave, astonishingly, everyone shuffled up to make room.

The table I picked, unwittingly, was the #WomenEd table. I had come across most of the #WomenEd team individually on social media, without realising the *connection*. They were women leaders of education who embodied everything I was trying to achieve. Hard-working, ethical women, who supported others relentlessly, and who wore their imperfections as proudly as I wore my newest pair of Doc Martens (red and sparkly; I figured if you're going to go full-on stompy, do it in style). Maybe it was karma as that herd of goats and #WomenEd were both included in the *tes* inaugural Top Ten Education Influencers in 2017:

'They are the people, campaigns and farmyard animals that have made a difference to education in England in 2017.' (George, 2017)

A GIRL-GUIDING FORCE

There was never the slightest hint of being anything other than welcomed, but make no mistake – it's no coffee morning. The #WomenEd *community* will support you and will also *challenge* your thinking, hold a mirror up to your avoidance techniques, and, most vitally, be a powerful force, gently pushing you forward, step by step, to be braver than you thought possible. They tell you it starts with 10%, but that's just the first step.

Since taking that first step outside of the comfort blanket of my school *community*, I have discovered two things:

- I am still alive.
- I have only just started my journey.

And I'm not alone. That's three things, I know, but the third thing is so many other things combined. It's the friends and colleagues I have met, it's the #SBLconnect movement in which we meet in real life. It's the fact that every day new voices appear in blogs, articles and on social media. It's the excitement with which I pitched to do a session at #WomenEd London unconference in March 2020 and succeeded. It's the courage it took me to run a nationwide survey into school business leader salaries and collate that information into a report which highlights the inequality in SBL pay and recognition (Goldsmith, 2019). It's the temerity it took to bang on the doors of trade unions, asking for a conversation about how to fix it, and the bravery to risk unpopularity by taking an assertive line when I feel my profession is being let down.

Passing on being 10% braver

- If you can visualise it, you can achieve it. Set small goals but keep on taking steps. Every day you'll be a little bit closer.

- Find yourself a big powerful bear to walk alongside you. I found #WomenEd; yours might be your professional body, an inspirational movement or a group of like-minded collaborators.

- Get yourself onto social media and make *connections*. Remember to speak as much as you listen and join the big conversations. No one will hear you if you're only talking to yourself.

- Accept and be honest about your fears and struggles. Our imperfections are what make us unique and interesting. Be as brave as you know you can be, be proud of everything you do, and, most of all, go and find your own happy.

REFERENCES

The Future Leaders Trust (2015) '1700 female headteachers 'missing' from England's schools, [Online]. Available at: https://s3.eu-west-2.amazonaws.com/ambition-institute/documents/1700_FEMALE_HEADS_MISSING_FROM_ENGLISH_SCHOOLS.pdf (accessed 5 November 2020). (accessed 13 August 2020).

George, M. (2017) 'The 10 most influential figures in education in 2017', *tes*, 22 December [Online]. Available at: www.tes.com/news/revealed-10-most-influential-figures-education-2017 (accessed 25 January 2020).

Goldsmith, H. (2019) School Business Leadership Salary Survey [Online]. Available at: www.sbl365.co.uk/salarysurvey (accessed at 25 January 2020).

Institute of School Business Leadership (ISBL) (2020) School Business Professional Workforce Survey Report 2020, 23 January [Online]. Available at: https://isbl.org.uk/home/Resource/ISBL%20WFS%20Guide%20Online%20Version.pdf (accessed 25 January 2020).

12

WHAT GOVERNORS AND TRUSTEES CAN DO TO BUILD DIVERSE AND INCLUSIVE WORKPLACES

Lesley Dolben and Natalie de Silva

KEY POINTS

This chapter will demonstrate how two women with protected characteristics:

- Enhanced their bravery and impact by working together and finding their voice;
- Discovered new ways to influence and advocate for *change* beyond headship;
- Championed diversity and inclusion within the school workforce as headteachers and governors.

INTRODUCTION

Lesley first became a governor more than 20 years ago. Two years ago, she joined the governing body of a large secondary school and is now governance lead for a multi-academy trust. Natalie found that she had the capacity to become a governor and trustee after leaving headship. We, Lesley and Natalie, started working together to advise schools in difficulty in 2016. Active engagement with governance has provided a platform for both of us to advocate for diversity and inclusive working practices in the schools we support.

In today's educational landscape, governors and trustees volunteer considerable time and expertise across the academy, state and independent sectors. Governors can be agents for *change* as they possess a unique ability to influence strategically. Governors and trustees are free from the constraints of complying with an employer's culture for fear of losing a role, and can, instead, become champions for *change*. In the most inclusive settings, governors and leaders work collaboratively to clearly define the school's vision and values and to drive the diversity and inclusion agenda and shared aspiration, with recognisable milestones along the way.

There were personal and practical reasons for us to press for greater diversity and inclusion. Within our roles as headteachers, governors and female leaders, we have both experienced inequality in terms of pay and opportunity within our careers. Facing hip replacement in 2016 and following cancer surgery, Lesley experienced first hand the many *challenge*s of disability in the workplace. Natalie, applying for senior leadership and then her first headship, was told many times that she was too young to be a senior leader. Both have had to *challenge* the lack of understanding of the power of inclusion and diversity to bring about effective school improvement and support workforce wellbeing.

FIGHTING FOR CHANGE BY WORKING WITH THE EQUALITIES ACT

In 2004, Lesley became the headteacher of a large primary school in Leeds. To tackle entrenched underperformance, Lesley worked to create an inclusive learning environment, sensitive to the cultural needs of its diverse learners. Following painstaking consultation, learning and sharing, Lesley and her governors carefully developed an 'Investors in Diversity' action plan (National Centre for Diversity, n.d.) with the whole school *community*. The outcomes included a wider curriculum, reasonable adjustments, such as single-sex swimming and ethos-based assemblies, a culturally appropriate lunch menu, and a multi-faith prayer room with washing facilities. Close working relationships with the local mosque enabled staff to share safeguarding training, and one of the madrassa classes was welcomed into the school building. It took courage for Lesley and her team of leaders to reach out to the *community* and model a more sensitive way of doing things.

Lesley brought this experience to her next role in a new school, endeavouring to advance equality and eliminate discrimination. Lesley and the governors reviewed staff structures and carried out impact assessments, including reviewing the gender, ethnicity and pay differentials. Reflecting on such practice, Lesley needed to be courageous in recommending and implementing a diverse staffing structure at a time when this was rarely seen. Natalie, entering headship ten years later, didn't need such courage as the recruitment process in her own schools was always inclusive. However, when Natalie was ready to leave executive headship and move to director level in a new trust, she was shocked to be informed by more than one recruitment consultant that as a young, ethnic minority woman, she was unlikely to succeed. She was told that such jobs went to older, white, Oxbridge-educated men. When Lesley first became a headteacher in 1997, she was the youngest female head in Lancashire. Mum to two small children, she was often the only woman in the room. Governors routinely enquired about child-care at interview and part-time or flexible working options were unheard of. At board level in 2020, Natalie still finds herself, as a young woman, facing many barriers, which limit remuneration and advancement.

Within school, many men are rapidly advanced to leadership positions, and many women are routinely left behind. The glass ceiling may be the result of years of social engineering leading to unconscious bias, which means that women can self-limit, but human resources processes need to share culpability. We argue that the need to build diverse and inclusive workplaces requires an honest examination of individual settings, and that governors, as *community* representatives, are best placed to broker this dialogue. The lack of proportionate representation of women at senior leadership and board level should be at the forefront of leaders' minds during recruitment and appraisal processes. Governors should seek to understand whether this intransigent and ever-growing gap applies within their own establishment.

SHAPING INCLUSION THROUGH VISION AND VALUES

Inclusive consultative processes that are sensitive in both design and delivery are an essential prerequisite when developing vision and values. In a largely EAL (English as an Additional Language) school, for example, innovative and thoughtful solutions promote engagement. The outcome of any consultation can provide *clarity* and feed into the business case for diversity and inclusion. When reviewing vision and values statements, how many of us can say that they've been used to inform recruitment decisions? In retrospect, we see that we could have done so much more as headteachers, so now, as governors, we are both being 10% braver.

WORKING WITH PROTECTED CHARACTERISTICS

Schools are becoming remarkably adept at managing inclusivity amongst pupils. Within the workforce, however, the inclusion of staff with a disability is practically unheard of beyond the office. There is a cost to inclusion; a financial one, in the provision of reasonable adjustments, and a human one because people need to shift their mindset around what is possible or even desirable. If we are serious about schools becoming reflective of society, then we need to find appropriate ways to support great teachers and leaders who also happen to have a disability. Lesley experienced first hand the *challenge*s of managing an unforgiving school building when she spent two years on crutches. It is possible when an individual is well supported, but, as we know, many disabilities are not visible. Natalie was once asked by governors what the point was in interviewing a primary teacher in a wheelchair; obviously, she interviewed the teacher anyway. The provision of accessible toilets for a teacher with coeliac disease, for example, also needs an additional adult to step in to provide cover. Inclusion needs to be appropriately funded in the workplace if it is to become a viable option. Is this possible in a school with today's budgetary constraints?

Whilst an individual's sexuality and religious preference are entirely private matters, the LGBTQ descriptors have proven challenging for some communities to accept, hence the need to embrace the No Outsiders curriculum to enhance awareness and remind all of their duties under the law (Moffat, 2017). Multi-faith Britain should also be reflected in our workplace provision. In 2004, a quiet space and washing facilities for ritual observance and prayer were thought of as unusual; not so today. Governors must support their headteachers in recognising bias, standing up to prejudice and being clear that their school *community* welcomes, champions and enables all staff to flourish for the benefit of the children served.

FLEXIBILITY IN THE WORKPLACE

An inclusive workplace is also a flexible one. Embracing the well-described business case for flexible working can better enable governors to champion its use. Both of us work flexibly (and successfully!) because our organisations support such innovative working practice, but many schools retain fixed ideas around curriculum delivery and leadership, and consequently struggle to accommodate requests. The risk to this fixed view is losing highly skilled and experienced teachers and leaders. In 2012, co-headship provided Lesley with a fascinating insight into a new way of working at executive level. Governors needed that extra 10% of courage to agree at first, however Lesley and her colleague brought very different energies and their combined impact proved transformative. Co-leadership opportunities are now being seen more often, and governors can be 10% braver in adopting such practices. #WomenEd, with partners, has collated a new set of case studies which show the benefits of flexible working for individuals, organisations and students (Chartered College of Teaching, n.d.). In order to advocate effectively for this, governors and senior leaders can draw on these case studies to appreciate the opportunity flexible working offers.

THE DIVERSITY BUSINESS CASE

The role of governor has grown exponentially over the years and comes with significant accountability. Given the responsibilities governors now assume, the pursuit of equalities is often stuck at the bottom of the to-do list. Diverse workforces reflect their communities and real life in Britain. Diversity promotes tolerance and understanding and a model for our pupils; it facilitates dialogue between communities and cultures and builds up a body of knowledge and respect for all. A well-described business case moves this issue beyond the moral imperative and can, of itself, become the *change* catalyst. There is a wealth of research describing the improved performance outcomes of diverse teams. Beyond the measurable increase in creativity, the positive human and reputational benefits of belonging to a truly inclusive workplace are worth highlighting (Kochan et al., 2003).

In order to empower ethical decision making, governors need to ensure that they are inclusive of all stakeholders and fully understand the potential unconscious bias in recruitment processes. Governors need to recognise that they must move beyond simple compliance to proactive, effective equalities monitoring. In today's multi-cultural Britain, the lack of ethnic diversity within education, particularly the representation of minority ethnic staff at senior level, ought to be of concern to all. The information gleaned from equalities monitoring should inform the targeted marketing of future posts. We don't see this happening in today's market. Is this because leaders don't have time, or is it not a priority for them?

As governors and trustees, we are struck by the generalised language in respect of the public sector equality duty; we feel governors and headteachers would benefit from further support and clarification. What does 'have due regard to...' (Government Equalities Office and Equality and Human Rights Commission, 2010, Chapter 1, para. 149) look like in practical terms? Building an inclusive workplace requires *change* to be driven incrementally through such things as adjusting recruitment processes, improving staff facilities, offering flexible and job-share working, and increasing access to professional learning. With careful planning, governors and trustees can find innovative and ethical ways (National Governance Association, n.d.) ways to attract and retain diverse teams and so build inclusive schools.

Passing on being 10% braver

- You don't have to be a headteacher to make a difference. Women can be 10% braver and make their voices heard beyond headship in many different spheres, such as chairing governing bodies and becoming trustees, which develop an alternative avenue for influence.

- Those of us who have experienced inequality in our careers can be powerful advocates for new and more inclusive ways of working. It takes courage to speak out and act as a role model and agent for *change*.

- The business rationale needs to be crystal clear for an inclusive school setting. All decisions that have financial drivers, as well as moral and ethical ones, are then more palatable for those reluctant to embrace *change*.

- Create opportunities for governor networking and peer review. Colleagues who support and *challenge* one another and share expertise will have their best practice disseminated more widely.

- Remember that inclusivity is a journey, not a destination: governors and school leaders need to be 10% braver, patient enough to believe this and courageous enough to allow for the inevitable cultural shifts that lead to success.

REFERENCES

Chartered College for Teaching (n.d.) Flexible Working [Online]. Available at: https://chartered.college/flexible-working/ (accessed 8 March 2020).

Government Equalities Office and Equality and Human Rights Commission (2010) Equality Act 2010: Guidance [Online]. Available at: www.gov.uk/guidance/equality-act-2010-guidance (accessed 28 March 2020).

Kochan, T., Bezrukova, K., Ely, R., Jackson, S., Joshi, A., Jehn, K., Leonard, J., Levine, D. and Thomas, D. (2003) 'The effects of diversity on business performance: Report of the diversity research network', *Human Resource Management*, 18 April [Online]. Available at: https://onlinelibrary.wiley.com/doi/abs/10.1002/hrm.10061 (accessed 28 March 2020).

Moffat, A. (2017) *No Outsiders in Our School: Teaching the Equality Act in Primary Schools*. London: Routledge.

National Centre for Diversity (n.d.) Investors in Diversity Award [Online]. Available at: https://nationalcentrefordiversity.com/diversity-accreditations/investors-in-diversity (accessed November 2019).

National Governance Association (n.d.) 'Ethical leadership for a better education system' [Online]. Available at: https://www.nga.org.uk/ethicalleadership.aspx (accessed 5 November 2020).

PART 3
BRAVING THE CHANGE

PART

3

13
RETIREMENT IS NOT A DIRTY WORD

Fiona McSorley

KEY POINTS

This chapter will:

- Encourage those nearing retirement to be 10% braver and celebrate it;
- Provide advice for those who may be feeling a little apprehensive (as I was) about making the final decision;
- Enable you to explore the new opportunities that exist to use your skills and expertise.

INTRODUCTION

Nobody talks about retirement. This has always puzzled me. It's not Fight Club, so why do people try to keep it such a secret? Why is it necessary to have hushed conversations with human resources staff as if no one should hear that you have decided to end your long, rewarding career in which you have educated thousands of young people? Surely this is a time for celebration, not secrecy.

In November 2018, 2.1% of the teacher workforce were aged over 60, meaning that there are over 9,600 people who may be considering retirement (DfE, 2019). With this, there is a danger of losing a valuable source of knowledge, skills and experience as teachers retire from the profession. We can't afford to do this, especially when recruitment is difficult. It's vital that school leaders recognise the importance of this step for their staff and support them along the way to a successful retirement. We also know that teachers are working longer as the pension age gets pushed back. Headteachers should be encouraged to look after their very experienced staff as they approach retirement, as well as ensuring there is a succession plan. To me, this means transferring those gems of knowledge to the new generation of education leadership. I retired in 2017 and was so pleased that one of my roles was taken over by a talented female teacher who had been one of my trainees at the start of her career.

I am in a privileged position to share my recent experiences and *challenge*s in the hope that people will start to talk about retirement, that they will prepare for a new phase in their lives and see it as a new beginning to be embraced. There are many ways to use your professional skills out in the wider world. The difference is that it becomes your choice of when, where and with whom.

BE PREPARED

Make the decision to retire at the right time for you. There is no one size that fits all. Your decision may be influenced by finance and the amount of pension you will receive, particularly if you have had breaks in your service. As a single parent, I had to be very aware of the need to pay my bills and provide for my daughter who is often too ill to work. Your decision may be based on your health as teaching can be exhausting and you want to ensure that there will be years ahead for you to enjoy. It may be influenced by other external factors such as looking after elderly parents. Or it could just be you have had enough. The timing of my decision was influenced by yet another educational *change* as I had no desire to learn a new set of GCSE and A-level specifications.

There is a lot of good guidance for the age that you can retire on the Teachers' Pensions website and particularly about the recent *change*s to the teachers' pension scheme. I highly recommend that you go on the website (www.teacherspensions.co.uk), register and look at the advice. The pension calculator allows you to enter different times for retirement so you can start to plan when it will be best for you financially. If you have *change*d authorities or employers, you should check that your pension is up to date and all your service is included. You can decide how much lump sum versus annual salary you wish to pay yourself. Again, this is a very personal decision, balancing the need to pay the bills with the delight of cash in hand!

CELEBRATE

Teachers are not normally great at singing their own praises, but this is the time to do it. How you let people know you are retiring is up to you, but please do not be shy about it – you have earned every comment, card or bunch of flowers (in my case orchids) that comes your way. I am not a party person, but I was determined to have a retirement party in the place where I seemed to spend most of my days – the sixth form common room – and I loved it. A summer's evening, a party playlist, cake and teachers and friends, old and new, made for very happy memories.

Saying goodbye to staff and students can be difficult, but make the time to do so. You cannot predict who or what you will miss the most, so make the best of the time and speak to as many people as you can. Leave as much detail about your role as possible for those who come after you; pass on folders, files, standard letters and lists of things to do. Being a great leader is about creating and empowering the leaders who succeed you.

WHAT NEXT?

For some, the first badly needed step is a holiday. Here is the benefit at last of taking a holiday in term time. It's cheaper and less busy, so do treat yourself. It may be the time for that long-haul flight to Australia or Canada, or simply to lie on that Greek beach.

This will not suit everyone and, on that first day in September when you no longer must dash about getting everything ready, you may feel a little lost. Retirement has many advantages – time to sleep, read books and catch up with old friends – but it can feel like you have lost your purpose. After all, you can no longer respond to that age-old question, 'what do you do?' with the proud reply 'I am a teacher'. So, find a new purpose. With so much knowledge and expertise, there is still a valued role for you in society.

You may want to consider the following options:

- Part-time work
- Paid consultancy work
- Voluntary work
- Looking after mind and body.

Some colleagues transition into retirement by taking part-time posts and then gradually reducing days and hours. This can help reduce the suddenness of stopping. It is also an opportunity to ensure that your wealth of knowledge and expertise can be inherited by the next generation of teachers and leaders coming through. You may need to share an examination class to ensure the subject continues, so that others learn from your experience of teaching the subject. It is also a way for the school to hang on to its valued staff for a little longer and prepare the way for their final retirement. However, schools should also remember to look after their pre-retirement teachers as much as possible with regards to their physical health and stamina.

I personally did not fancy supply, which is another alternative, but know some retired teachers who do the occasional day. For others, a clean break is needed. Leaving a school is like being homesick. There are the people to miss as well as routines. I still think of my day in hour periods and wonder when half term is. But times *change* and a new guard takes over, so it's best to let them get on with it.

I was fortunate to be recruited by a school improvement organisation, to continue to work with schools and support their sixth forms. This means that, from the other side of the table, I can help people sitting where I had sat for many years, listen to their woes and offer my help and advice. The additional income is always welcome but mainly keeps up my contact with schools. I do know people who have successfully set up their own consultancies and use their expertise through supporting school improvement and conferences. They make use of their contacts in education and work it around other aspects of their retirement lives.

BEING 10% BRAVER

My 10% braver story comes from volunteer work as a trustee at my local multi-academy trust (MAT). I had hoped to become a governor and pay back the support I had received, but finding a place was difficult through the government portal. I took it upon myself to write to local schools and was offered the role of trustee/director at my small, local MAT. This was a big *challenge* for me, to step even further back and look at the big picture of several schools. It is not easy as most of the board discussions centre around finance rather than education. Schools are also very different entities and quite idiosyncratic, so my secondary experience does not always fit other schools. With my training background, I was determined to improve my skills and found a great governance leadership course through Ambition School Leadership/Confederation of School Trusts. The distance-learning modules are very useful, and I was given a mentor who gave me encouragement and sound advice on the difficult transition from senior leadership team to multi-academy trust board. It is still very challenging; I don't like the politics, but my education background is valued and I am now the vice chair.

My role as a network leader for #WomenEd in London gives me the opportunity to give back and support the next generation of school leaders. I can support the *community* and spread the word wherever I am able. People come up to me at conferences and frequently ask me about #WomenEd and my role, and I am happy to encourage them to join us. It is important that I continue to promote the message in as many different forums as I can.

MIND AND BODY

Ageing does bring its problems. One of the contributing reasons to retire was the deterioration in my hearing (hereditary) so looking after yourself is important. Get that free flu jab. Join a club or class, and swim, do yoga or Pilates. It's a good way to meet other people and keep mobile. Take a walk regularly and invest time in yourself. Get a free travel pass, if available, and visit places/art galleries/museums that you never had time for before. The railcard for over-60s gives you 30% off train tickets, which is great for mid-week getaways to visit friends and family. As I no longer spend Sundays working, I was able to go back to attending church and reconnected with a lovely *community* and people I had not seen in years. I joined the church choir and, again, it's a *challenge* to read music and sing different parts, but I have met wonderful friends and, maybe, am just a little bit proud of myself.

Passing on being 10% braver

- Plan ahead for retirement, be brave and ask for advice from others or professionals. It does not have to be a secret.

- Celebrate your career. You have earned that party and all those thank you cards!

- Be brave enough to continue to use your skills and knowledge so that the stop is not too sudden and you still have a role.

- Look out for opportunities that give a sense of belonging and offer that mental or physical *challenge* that will keep you learning.

REFERENCE

Department for Education (DfE) (2019) School Workforce in England: November 2018, 27 June [Online]. Available at: https://assets.publishing.service.gov.uk/government/uploads/system/uploads/attachment_data/file/811622/SWFC_MainText.pdf (accessed 3 April 2020).

14
RETURNING TO TEACHING AND LEADERSHIP AFTER ILLNESS

Rachael Paget

KEY POINTS

This chapter will:

- demonstrate how illness fundamentally *changed* me as an individual;
- show how I was 10% braver in returning to work.

INTRODUCTION

I knew I needed to reassess things when I woke up after nine days in a medically induced coma and my first words were 'I'm going to get in trouble; I never set cover!' My family were delighted as I was conscious, with the danger of brain damage avoided. All I felt was panic, confusion and a burning desire to return to my classroom. Along with this was an all-consuming fear: what if I never teach again?

Little did I know it, but over the next nine months I had to employ the #WomenEd mantra and be 10% braver until I managed to return to my beloved classroom.

WHAT HAPPENED TO ME?

At 32 I had my first asthma attack. It was so severe I was rushed via ambulance to Accident & Emergency. The medical team placed me into a medically induced coma to get my breathing under control which took over a week.

Whilst I was in the Intensive Care Unit, I also developed hospital-acquired pneumonia and an ischemic bowel with multiple perforations, leading to emergency bowel surgery and the fitting of two temporary stomas. If that wasn't dramatic enough, I was given such strong medication that I lost muscle strength and tone and had to work hard with physiotherapists to regain my ability to get out of bed, sit in a chair, stand up and walk. I spent over five weeks in the hospital and another eight months rehabilitating before starting my phased return to work.

I will be eternally grateful to the National Health Service for saving my life, but my major motivating factor when learning to cope and regain my mobility was returning to the classroom. Teaching is my vocation. I knew that I would not be happy until I was back teaching.

I viewed my return to work as a staircase, a series of steps that I would slowly climb until I was working full time as an English teacher and had reclaimed my leadership responsibility for teaching and learning. It started by simply getting into school. That itself was tiring and anxiety inducing but my school gave me time to reacclimatise. The school understood the importance of *communication*. We planned my return together: from getting me into the building and then the classroom as an observer, to team teaching with the teacher who had covered my role. This was difficult occasionally, requiring a careful balance of two different teaching styles, but it was also helpful as it enabled me to get to know my classes with support if needed. I built my teaching time up slowly, over seven weeks, until I was back.

My experience taught me that phased returns are vital and must be done properly. They should be individualised and created in dialogue with the person who is returning to work. If you are ever in the position where you need a phased return to work, do not be afraid to advocate for what you need. You know yourself and your health best. You are the expert. A phased return is about facilitating your return to work, so if that means that things need to be done at a certain pace, or with certain conditions, don't be afraid to ask for them. As Whitmell (2014) states, 'explaining to your manager how to recognise symptoms of illness means they can then offer concrete help.'

Remember that a referral to Occupational Health is worth considering to discuss your current and ongoing needs. It's also important to note that there will be bumps in the road. To accept this takes bravery. It can also generate feelings of frustration. I had several bump-in-the-road moments. It is an emotional time. Don't be afraid to be open and honest with your line manager and those facilitating your return to work. *Communication* is key.

IF YOU BECOME ILL, HOW SHOULD YOU BE TREATED?

Compassionately. It sounds so obvious, but it is amazing how many horror stories there are where this didn't happen. Mary Myatt was right: we are 'human beings first, professionals second' (2016: 13). Nobody chooses to become ill. I'll say that again for those that are struggling: nobody chooses to become ill. Illness is not a sign of moral weakness, a character flaw or a conscious decision. It is a twist of fate and an inconvenience. The person that is most inconvenienced by it all is the person who is ill. This is where we must keep things in perspective and remove our egos.

Andy Sammons is correct in his book, *The Compassionate Teacher*: we need to place 'compassion at the heart of everything we do' (2019: 19). When we are focused on the minutiae of school life, we must not forget this, no matter how difficult it is.

Ultimately, as teachers, and especially as leaders, we must exercise compassion towards our students, our colleagues and ourselves. It's about dignity, trust and motivation, all of which are enhanced when we are treated with compassion. Our profession deals with and in humanity and this needs to be at the forefront of everything we do, decide or deliver.

HOW TO GET BACK IN THE GAME

Know your rights and responsibilities

Whether you are the person returning to work, or the person facilitating someone's phased return, it is important to be aware of the rights and responsibilities you have around this area. Get advice from HR or your union if necessary. There is no such thing as a stupid question. We're not legal experts, so it's important to seek out expert advice to ensure everything is done correctly. Remember that there will be no one more loyal and hardworking than a staff member who feels that they are supported and able to have honest, open *communication* with their managers.

Under the Equality Act 2010, all employers are required to make 'reasonable adjustments' to prevent their employees and job applicants being placed at any disadvantage. The problem is that what this actually means is open to interpretation, as 'legislation does not require their organisations to make every adjustment employees might ask for' (Murray, 2013). However, open *communication*, in my experience, assures that compromises can be found. Remember, 'resilience is about being an active participant' (Erasmus, 2019: 41).

Expect changes

It is important to remember that people and institutions *change*. Illness will have probably *change*d you; it certainly *change*d me. And, in your absence, *change*s will have occurred within your school. Give yourself time to find your feet and to absorb the *change*s. As Kate Murray says, it can be a 'testing time' (2013). We sometimes forget that the school has continued in our absence.

Don't be afraid to ask for details of policy *change*s; I certainly needed this. Thanks to some careful planning and *collaboration* between my principal, my director of learning and myself, my first week of phased return was based in the departmental office, allowing me to reacclimatise and familiarise myself with these new policies and procedures.

Confidence is key

Kay and Shipman have written much about women's 'acute lack of *confidence*' (2014), but I think it's also relevant when discussing a return to work after illness. Most people who have been off for a prolonged period suffer a crisis of *confidence* and begin to doubt themselves and their abilities. It's important to be aware of this: when it happens, you can reassure yourself that it is normal to feel this way and it isn't representative of a lack of ability or that you've finally been found out. I certainly felt this. I am naturally an anxious person, so add to this my post-traumatic stress disorder as a result of the medical experiences and I was frightened returning to work. The department had understandably moved on without me, the dynamics had *changed* and it was difficult to find my place in the new order. I had naively assumed that everything would just go back to the way it had been, but how could it? One thing that I found helped me was counselling and cognitive behavioural therapy. This gave me the skills to cope with and *challenge* my more intrusive and negative thoughts. Therapy is hard work, but I recommend it to everyone, not just those who have experienced traumatic events. Another thing that helped me was remembering Sue Cowley's advice on *confidence*: 'Building your *confidence* can be about using a quiet inner strength to make your way through the world' (2019: 19).

As women, historically we have had a culture of minimising our successes or deflecting praise. #WomenEd is beginning to break that down and it's about time! One of the best ideas I have heard to help combat this was at a #WomenEd event in Leeds, West Yorkshire in July 2019, when Dr Tamsin Bowers-Brown spoke eloquently about the idea of 'boast buddies', women who celebrate each other's successes because they struggle to celebrate their own. Since then I have become an active boast buddy for lots of fellow teachers both in school and online. I also have my own boast buddies who remind me of how far I have come whenever I have a wobble or moment of self-doubt.

FINDING YOUR COMMUNITY CAN HELP

People often berate social media, yet it can be a force for good. I have found great support in online communities that have helped me come to terms with my disabilities, empowered me to advocate for myself and see that I am not alone. #WomenEd is a huge source of support and inspiration for me, especially as it is an inclusive movement. Through discovering #WomenEd, I also found #DisabilityEd, a cross-over *community* equally as empowering and supportive. There is immense power and support to be found in intersectionality.

Becoming an active member of the teaching *community* beyond my own school has built my knowledge, *confidence* and networks. I will always be a disabled teacher: now I realise that there is power in embracing this. This power enables you to be 10% braver and 100% your authentic self. When you accept and embrace yourself fully, you will find that others do too.

THERE IS STRENGTH IN VISIBILITY

This next piece of advice is not for everyone, but I have found that there is strength in visibility. I am happy to discuss my disabilities with colleagues and students who ask me questions.

I may have disabilities that are, for the most part, invisible, but I am happy to be visible. I use a desk slope when marking to ease the strain on my hypermobile wrists. I use my crutch, wrist splints, thumb splints, joint supports and compression gloves as and when I need them. My inhaler sits in all its bright pink glory on my desk and students know that they do not spray anything in or near my classroom. In embracing my identity as a teacher with a disability, I have found *confidence* and strength in myself as an individual, a teacher and a leader. This has enabled me to be 10% braver and embrace more opportunities; it even led to me sharing my story in this chapter – something I would never have been brave enough to do before! Megan Dalla-Camina's (2018) wise words on overcoming imposter syndrome have become a bit of a mantra for me: 'You are here for a reason. In this job, your business, your life, you are worthy.'

Passing on being 10% braver

- *Communication* is key - be brave and speak openly about what you need.
- Find your *community*, whether that's in school or online, as support is out there.
- *Change* is inevitable but not necessarily negative. Be aware that illness *changes* people and that schools develop and *change* rapidly. Allow people time to become reacquainted.
- Own your journey and your story.

REFERENCES

Cowley, S. (2019) '10% braver: Feel the fear and do it anyway', in V. Porritt and K. Featherstone (eds), *10% Braver: Inspiring Women to Lead Education*. London: Sage, pp. 15–24.

Dalla-Camina, M. (2018) 'The reality of imposter syndrome', *Psychology Today*, 3 September [Online]. Available at: www.psychologytoday.com/us/blog/real-women/201809/the-reality-imposter-syndrome (accessed 29 October 2019).

Erasmus, C. (2019) *The Mental Health + Wellbeing Handbook for Schools: Transforming Mental Health Support on a Budget*. London and Philadelphia, PA: Jessica Kingsley.

Kay, K. and Shipman, C. (2014) 'The *confidence* gap', *The Atlantic*, May [Online]. Available at: www.theatlantic.com/magazine/archive/2014/05/the-confidence-gap/359815 (accessed 29 October 2019).

Murray, K. (2013) 'Returning to work after illness: What support do employees need?', *The Guardian*, 30 May [Online]. Available at: www.theguardian.com/careers/returning-work-illness-support-employees (accessed 25 October 2019).

Myatt, M. (2016) *High Challenge, Low Threat: Finding the Balance*. Woodbridge: John Catt Educational.

Sammons, A. (2019) *The Compassionate Teacher: Why Compassion Should Be at the Heart of our Schools*. Woodbridge: John Catt Educational.

Whitmell, C. (2014) 'Returning to work after mental health issues: Tips for transition', *The Guardian*, 27 January [Online]. Available at: www.theguardian.com/careers/careers-blog/returning-to-work-after-mental-health-issues (accessed 28 October 2019).

15

BEING AN INTERNATIONAL SCHOOL LEADER

Liz Free with Sue Aspinall, Ruth Barsby and Pauline O'Brien

KEY POINTS

This chapter will:

- Explore the experiences of aspiring and existing international women leaders;
- Show how they found the *confidence* to be uncertain whilst living in a global world;
- Provide advice to encourage more women to make the brave leap into international school leadership.

INTRODUCTION

There are over 11,000 international schools in the world, which employ over half a million staff and educate over five million students (ISC Research, 2019). This sector had 2,000 schools in 2000, with predictions placing the global market at 20,000 schools by 2029. If these forecasts are accurate, we'll need an additional half a million teachers to make the bold leap into the #GlobalProfession. This equates to 1:4 teachers from the UK, the USA, Australia and Ireland, working internationally every year. And leaders will be needed so opportunity abounds.

I first became an international school leader in 2006 as, being 10% braver, I strove boldly into an international school headship at the British School of Boston, USA. Subsequently, I've worked throughout the world, now with a family firmly at my side. However, when I look back to this first posting I shudder at what I didn't ask and how little I knew. Whilst the potential is very exciting, becoming an international school leader requires contractual awareness (in ways I hadn't conceived!), openness and the willingness to be *challenged* and to *challenge*.

In this chapter, we'll explore the experiences of women leaders through their personal stories and reflections alongside advice for those looking to make the leap.

SUE ASPINALL, #WOMENED NETHERLANDS CO-FOUNDER AND EXECUTIVE HEADTEACHER

I started my career in the public sector in England's diverse and vibrant schools where I learnt what excellent learning, teaching and leading look like. These experiences have framed my decisions ever since.

I was attracted to the international sector as I could combine a love of travel with continuing my own professional development. In August 2006, after being a deputy head for seven years, I set out to secure a headship overseas.

To move out of the public into the private sector takes soul searching and guts. My critics and self-talk kept reminding me that I'd be living amongst the affluent expat world, the globe-trotting elite. I needed to be courageous and believe that I could make a difference in this strange system and align my moral conscience.

My search for the right school focused on vacancies appearing in *tes*. I prepared my CV, drafted a letter and applied for the schools that seemed to fit my needs. My criteria list then was basic; now I would do more research through my networks. At the time, I had little to reference and went more on gut and intuition.

I had interviews in Central London led by respective heads of school. The good thing about this approach is that you can decide immediately whether you can work with this person. If in doubt, pull out.

The job I accepted was in Japan and I went to Tokyo for the final two-day interview. I remember the feeling of 'other worldliness' that hit me during that visit. Coming face to face with the extraordinary bombardment of sensory stimulation of Tokyo was exciting and overwhelming. It was obvious from my tour of the school and observing lessons that significant improvements were needed for the school to succeed as a reputable education provider and a business. Without a love for karaoke, sushi and sake, I wondered if I would have a life beyond school.

On starting my role, the senior team and I created the school improvement road map; it wasn't easy. There were naysayers, 'old boys' and 'diehards' who made me question what I was doing. But there were also the most remarkable professional, talented staff, who all shared a journey which culminated in an 'excellent' inspection after our first four years.

As a primary headteacher, I've always been managed by a head of school or CEO. They have always been male, ex-secondary headteachers, usually in the twilight of their careers. I learnt the hard way to manage banter, to *challenge* being excluded, to find my voice at board meetings and to use humour to respond to put-downs.

I remember blindly trusting the head of school, who recruited me for the position in Japan. In recent years, I have carefully checked and re-negotiated my draft contracts, ensured that my starting salary matches my experience and set out my non-negotiables. I have learnt that, in international leadership, you are entering a business and your tenure is vulnerable.

It is possible to make a career in international leadership and to do this alone, with a partner or a family. In every country I lived, I met women in similar situations to my own. You need to reach out, be brave, speak to anyone and network. You'll be amazed; this unique experience will stretch and mould you and take you to places, both real and metaphorical, that you never thought possible.

RECRUITING INTERNATIONALLY

Pauline O'Brien, Director of Administrative Searches and Governance Services, International School Services (ISS)

International leadership posts are frequently advertised ahead of domestic system recruitment, with headship and principal roles being advertised up to two years ahead of appointment. It's important to understand the process to optimise your opportunities.

Planning for success

- Ensure your documentation is professional, up to date, clear and concise. The volume of applications means you must stand out for the right reasons. Try the STAR method (Situation, Task, Actions, Results) to describe your career path and your impact on student learning. Ensure all relevant information is in your CV as everyone reads this first and then decides whether to read the application letter. Don't be humble: explaining your achievements factually is essential!

- Understand the job requirements for the role and don't make assumptions as each school is different. Research shows that women typically wait until they have 100% of the requirements, whereas men apply once they have about 60% (Shipman, 2014). Although an advertisement may have set requirements, this can be an unrealistic wishlist. Boards will accept candidates with most but not all their requirements. They want to see that most of the requirements match your background, experience, skill and passion. They want to see what you will bring to their school and how your background is relevant to their future.

- Know yourself and your why! Ensure the job requirements match your values and ethos. The school and *community* must be a good fit as determined by such factors as strategic plan, governance structure, financial health of the school, student population, diversity, inclusion and wellbeing programmes, along with the cultural competence of students and staff. Will the people in your life be happy there too?

- Know your worth! Women make highly competent leaders and succeed in higher level positions just as much as men, so remuneration should be commensurate to the skill set required and not the gender. Spend time researching the package on offer and speak about skills and expertise when negotiating, not gender. CIS surveys its member schools and has identified a 23% gender pay gap (COIS, 2020). This is clearly an issue for boards as they consider packages. We need to work harder to remove unconscious bias around women earning less than men. Know your value to secure the most competitive, fair package to match the job.

- As most first interviews are conducted through technology platforms, become proficient in speaking to the tiny dot on your laptop. Make eye contact with the interviewer/s even if you don't see them. Often, you appear on a big screen in a meeting room so be aware of your body language and gestures – oh, and what the panellists see in your background.

THE BIG QUESTIONS

Ruth Barsby, international school teacher

Ruth made the leap into international education in 2019 after a career in the UK. She contacted me when considering her future path and documented the big questions that she had through this journey.

How and where is the best place to look for jobs in an international setting?

Many schools historically use *tes*, whilst a smaller number use *The Guardian* and global recruitment companies including CIS, Search Associates, Teach Away, Teach Anywhere and Gatenby Sanderson. Check the websites of international curriculum and membership organisations such as the International Baccalaureate Organization (IBO), the Education Collaborative of International Schools (ECIS) and the Council of British International Schools (COBIS).

Do I need additional qualifications before applying?

Generally, reputable international schools want teaching staff with Qualified Teacher Status (from their home country) and a track record of high performance and impact. For the American system and some contexts, a Masters-level degree (or equivalent) is helpful. They will look at aptitude to work in different contexts and openness to changing environments. Highlighting ongoing professional development and learning is a must.

How do you make progress and gain experience in international schools?

International schools invest significantly in their staff, more so than domestic systems. You can negotiate access to CPD such as higher-level study, National Professional Qualifications in school leadership (now available internationally) and executive leadership programmes. If you are considering moving internationally, use social media to reach out to leaders already in international schools. Ruth, who prepared these questions, contacted me online to discuss what it was really like before she applied. She even visited the Netherlands on holiday to find out about types of schools, processes, the important questions. The #WomenEd global network is a great place to start; reach out, connect and find out as much as possible.

How does the interview process work for an international school?

There isn't one uniform process. There will often be an interview electronically. The second round will likely happen at the school if appointing within Europe. If appointing for Asia/Middle East, it may be a centralised interview through a major recruitment fair or often in a hotel in a major city.

There will usually be several staff recruiting. Many reputable schools are a member of an accredited body such as CIS or COBIS; look for a copy of their latest accreditation visit on their website or the membership organisation website. If successful, you'll be made an offer: please read the contract thoroughly. Check the full package details, including salary, pension, CPD commitments if negotiated, healthcare, housing terms and value of the housing (if part of the package) and arrangements for repatriation during and at the end of your contract.

Are British schools inspected by Ofsted?

The short answer is no. Anyone can call themselves a British school (bizarrely). If you are specifically looking at British international schools, check the COBIS website (there is also FOBISIA and BSME) and whether they've had a British Schools Overseas (BSO) inspection. This means that they have been voluntarily inspected by a Department for Education-recognised inspectorate (such as ISI) against the British Schools Overseas standard. These schools can also offer the Newly Qualified Teacher induction process and a British-recognised education. If the school you are looking at doesn't have a recent inspection/accreditation visit, look closely at their academic outcomes, accountability measures and policies for teaching and learning. They may be offering amazing education opportunities, but have a closer look before committing to a role.

Is it affordable to move abroad?

Check your contract and cost of living comparison websites. Most reputable schools will offer full relocation but with limits on how much you can ship/fly in terms of overall weight/size and on items that you can bring into certain countries. Full repatriation should be offered but, again, check the fine print and request a sample salary listing the expected tax and take-home pay.

How long are the contracts to move internationally?

Contracts are rarely permanent. They are usually two years for teaching and middle/senior leadership positions and up to five years for headship. Most schools have an early notification period so you should know within two terms of end of contract whether it will be renewed and, equally, whether you wish to renew. This offers you lots of flexibility, but it can lead to some insecurity.

ADVICE TO THE PROSPECTIVE INTERNATIONAL SCHOOL LEADER

Having taken this leap twice in my professional career, as a single headteacher and as a married mum with two young children in a director role, I would unreservedly advise colleagues to work internationally at least once in their career. 71% of those leaving will return within 10 years, most within 3–4 years (COBIS, 2019), so this can be an adventure within a career. By being braver, we have all broadened, deepened and explored global practice as educators whilst expanding our personal horizons.

The consistent message from the fabulous women who contributed to this chapter is that you must do your homework, ensure the school matches your philosophy and negotiate your package. Do not take the first offer. You can negotiate relocation, flight allowances, salary, CPD, title, teaching load, and school fees for dependents. You also need a plan for what happens if it goes well and if you decide to return after your initial contract term. If you can, I advise that you keep property in your home country, so you have roots for your future. Plan for possible eventualities, and be happy with the unknown and the potential of an awesome adventure.

#WomenEd is a truly global network so reach out, reach wide and reach far. We are all here to support each other and to welcome more inspiring women leaders into this dynamic and evolving #GlobalProfession.

REFERENCES
COBIS (2019) Final Report and Case Studies: Teacher Supply in British International Schools [Online]. Available at: www.cobis.org.uk/cobis-news/news-detail/~post/final-report-and-case-studies-teacher-supply-in-british-international-schools-20180712 (accessed 1 November 2019).

COIS (2020) Asking the Right Questions: Gender Gap Revealed in Pay for International School Leaders [Online]. Available at: www.cois.org/about-cis/news/post/~board/

perspectives-blog/post/asking-the-right-questions-gender-gap-revealed-in-pay-for-international-school-leaders (accessed 1 December 2019).

ISC Research (2019) Homepage [Online]. Available at: www.iscresearch.com (accessed 30 October 2019).

Shipman, K. (2014) 'The *confidence* gap', *The Atlantic*, May [Online]. Available at: www.theatlantic.com/magazine/archive/2014/05/the-*confidence*-gap/359815 (accessed 6 November 2019).

16

A SMALL FISH IN A BIG POND: EDUCATIONAL LEADERSHIP OUTSIDE OF A SCHOOL ENVIRONMENT

Lizana Oberholzer

KEY POINTS

This chapter will:

- Outline the process of moving from a supportive school *community* to a higher education context;
- Show why I needed to be brave, have agency and lead with courage;
- Show how I developed and communicated my vision and passion to help others and embraced the 10% braver philosophy.

INTRODUCTION

For me, it was always a driving ambition to move from a school context to a broader context, and I felt that a natural next step was to progress to higher education (HE). I had always imagined that you progress from being a schoolteacher to leading in a school, and from there to become a teacher educator. I was fortunate enough to train teachers in my previous school context and was the director of a School Centred Initial Teacher Training (SCITT) course. The ability to engage with research to help refine practice was something that drew me to HE. The fact that I could work closely with future teachers to help children to become the best they can be was a huge motivating factor. I was determined to make a difference and impact positively on the communities I serve from a larger platform.

MAKING THE LEAP

The time came when it felt right to be 10% braver to take the leap into the unknown, to take on the next *challenge*. My goal was always to take on a new *challenge* after the SCITT's successful Ofsted, and the SCITT sailed through its inspection with flying colours. It was a very proud moment for the SCITT team and I when the 2015 report highlighted that the commitment and vision of the team were a real strength. To be honest, I was not sure how to progress or move on, or how to even apply for roles at HE level. I looked at application forms asking whether I had published, and what my research interest was. It is fair to say that the initial step to move on to my new role was taken rather naively. Unlike what Francke (2019) describes as women's reluctance to apply for roles where they don't feel they meet all the specified criteria, I, for once, took the leap to apply for something where I only met most of the criteria. I didn't have any publications, apart from work I shared in my own subject area, and, apart from my professional doctorate, focusing on early career teachers and mentoring and coaching, I did not have much to say about my research interest. I was a practitioner. I had to learn how to become an academic.

I landed the job, as the programme lead for School Direct, and my celebrations were short but sweet before the *challenge* started. It became clear that what initially had been perceived as my dream job also meant that, despite all my skills, I reverted back to being a novice (Dreyfus and Dreyfus, 1986) due to the new context in which I found myself. I understood how to run a school-based course, but I had very little knowledge about the HE context within which I now worked. Schools are fast-moving places and *change* can happen more quickly than it does at HE level. I had to learn to adjust, and to understand new jargon, new systems, a new pace and a different perspective on teacher development. The principles are the same but executed very differently.

I felt safe and supported in my school context, I had a group of supportive colleagues and I was established in terms of my expertise and skills. Moving to a context where I felt part of something bigger also led to isolation, and situations where I had to demonstrate that I had the knowledge, experience and skill set to contribute.

Cameron and Green (2012) highlight how leaders can drive individual, group and institutional *change*; however, once I moved beyond the sphere of my school, I had to do the work regarding individual *change*, and I had to grow. I realised it wasn't going to be easy to find my feet in a landscape that appeared similar to what I knew but was vastly different. I had to be 10% braver daily, to continue to engage with the role, and not to feel like I did not belong. All the *confidence* gained from a positive Ofsted outcome in my previous context disappeared in a second. I had to fall back on the wonderful friendships, *community* and support of the women at #WomenEd to guide me through the journey. I had to find ways to give myself agency to lead again, to be brave and support others. Sometimes just turning up was 10% braver. Admitting to it now is absolutely 10% braver.

INDIVIDUAL CHANGE

In the first few months in my new role, I realised that I was working my way through the development levels of the Dreyfus Model (Dreyfus and Dreyfus, 1986).

Despite having experience and skills, I needed to learn how to engage with the landscape, learn how to speak the language of the teams I worked with. I had to learn how to step into their shoes, and to listen with an intention to understand their world more effectively. It was important to transform individually to enable me to function well, and work effectively with others. As Dreyfus and Dreyfus (1986) suggest, the journey is often more accelerated for those with more experience; I soon managed to catch up and understand more about the context in which I found myself. Being brave meant that I had to understand my starting point, accept that I needed to build on my expertise, and admit that I needed help. The latter was hard as I was so used to knowing my job inside out, that it was alien to me to have to ask what to do, and how.

Collaborative professionalism was imperative to help me to find my way in this complex landscape (Hargreaves and O'Connor, 2018). I realised that the only way to understand the complexity of my new landscape fully was to start joining networks to help me reshape my understanding. I joined Athena Swan which is a charter managed by the UK Equality Challenge Unit which advocates for gender equality in HE, and I have the privilege to be a network leader for the #WomenEd team in London: these two organisations remain a continued support for me, at both my lowest moments and when celebrating success.

The HE comprised of a diverse *community*. Three years ago, I supported #BAMEed by offering to host their first London conference at my university. I was asked to support on the steering group, and I developed a greater understanding of how to support British, Asian, Minority Ethnic (BAME) educators on their journey as teachers through this. My involvement enabled me to see how I could be of service by offering coaching and mentoring support. The more I interacted with the different networks beyond my HE context, the more I gained an understanding of how to shape a vision for newly qualified teachers (NQTs) for #WomenEd.

I noticed that, like more experienced women in education, NQTs mirror similar characteristics in terms of the *confidence* gap, and this pattern seems even more pronounced for British Minority Ethnic (BME) groups (Francke, 2019).

I have always championed NQTs and early career teachers (ECTs) probably because I personally found it so challenging to find my feet as an ECT. My aim was to provide mentoring and coaching support for NQTs, initially locally in London, and to create an opportunity for NQTs to network with other like-minded colleagues in education via #WomenEd and an NQT unconference. The thinking was to encourage NQTs to become part of a lifelong supportive *community* where they can network and be collaborative professionals. The aim was to make the #WomenEd ethos of support a habit from the outset of the NQT journey as a new teacher. I was determined to help women to develop agency and authenticity, to have courage and be the best versions of themselves (Brown, 2018; Francke, 2019).

Through my own individual *change* journey, learning to progress from novice to competent and proficient practitioner in a different landscape, I was able to identify a specific need, and, with the help of #WomenEd leaders, I shaped a clear vision to launch the first #WomenEd NQT unconference in London, and to offer mentoring and coaching opportunities for NQTs.

SHARING THE VISION

The *challenge* was to share this vision with the wider education *community*, to ensure that I was able to get the project off the ground.

The clarity of the vision was vital. I realised that I needed to share this message consistently, on a local level, and to connect with other networks, via schools, Initial Teacher Training providers, teaching schools, and on an individual level. There was overwhelming support to share the message with others, particularly where #WomenEd *community* members were present, and who shared the message with passion and enthusiasm. I had to work hard to build the momentum in contexts where there was gender balance fatigue, or where the perception was that the 'women need fixing' (Francke, 2019). I had to outline the value of how, if we do have more women in leadership or confidently working within education, it will benefit both the school and the learners. I shared Francke's (2019) outline of the business case, with school leaders overseeing NQT and ECT support. The case is based on McKinsey's 2015 data which suggests that if there is true gender balance in the workplace, it could add $28 trillion total net return to the global gross domestic product (GDP), which is more than the USA and China's GDP combined.

This certainly puts the importance of the case in perspective! I stressed that we need confident women in schools to model best practice, and, by supporting NQTs from the outset, we not only empower them but also continue to offer support to retain them for the profession.

It required enthusiasm, a consistent message, and drive. It was clear that how the message is delivered made all the difference to how it is received. Sending emails or messages on different platforms was not enough to ensure that school leaders supported the vision. I had to ensure that I spoke to as many colleagues as possible in a wide educational landscape.

I realised that I need to have a consistent message and a clear vision, to connect with people and to ensure I build trusting relationships (Blanchard et al., 2013). We have now completed our third year of the #WomenEd NQT unconference and it continues to grow. You can see the video of the event on #WomenEd's YouTube Channel (https://youtu.be/39sEALN7mBw)

MOVING FROM INDIVIDUAL CHANGE TO GROUP CHANGE

Throughout this process of leading *change*, I had to work on my own development to adjust to my new context. I had to work with others, individually, to move to a position where small groups bought into the NQT project's vision (Cameron and Green, 2012). Developing strong and supportive networks were key to the success of the project (Hargreaves and O'Connor, 2018). However, what became clear is that such a project requires small incremental steps and milestones, to ensure that the *change* leads to permanence (Beabout, 2012). The project offered clear solutions to support school leaders to retain their staff and to support them in their development via #WomenEd's support. It offered opportunities where high *challenge* is presented to bridge the gender gap, but low threat, where the benefits far outweigh the *challenge*s (Myatt, 2016).

EMPOWERING OTHERS

Through the #WomenEd NQT project, I saw how NQTs became more empowered. NQTs shared how they *challenge*d the situations they faced in educational contexts, ranging from negotiating their working hours, through inappropriate comments in the workplace to discussing their starting salary. They no longer felt they lacked a voice and had to conform to what was expected of them. The power of working in a wider education *community* not only benefitted me but others too. Through their empowerment, I became more empowered and committed to the cause.

THE #WOMENED VALUES

When developing and leading the #WomenEd NQT initiative, I worked closely with Vivienne Porritt and she guided me to closely follow the #WomenEd values. We ensured that there was *clarity* regarding the vision and how to communicate it to others.

The aim was to provide clear *change*, by allowing NQTs to be part of a supportive *community* from the outset of their new careers, and to drive *change* whereby NQTs in the #WomenEd *community* develop *confidence* and a voice to flourish in the profession.

Passing on being 10% braver

Moving education contexts, from a school to a university in my case, *challenged* me to reflect on how I needed to adopt a mindset where I could *challenge* the norm. As Einstein states: 'The world as we have created it is a process of our thinking. It cannot be *change*d without changing our thinking' (cited in Thomas-EL et al., 2019: 35).

The insights I draw from my own experience are as follows:

- I had to be brave to allow myself to be a novice in a new context.

- I had to learn how I could have agency again to lead and to make a difference.

- I had to learn how to draw on the supportive networks around me to convey strong visions, to help others to develop and succeed.

- Through the learning of others and their and my success, I became braver every day for them and for myself to continue to drive *change*.

It is important that women in education continue to drive *change* with conviction and commitment. We need to guard against 'gender-balance fatigue' and continue to work on making a difference for our communities (Francke, 2019). Being 10% braver has become a philosophy and a way of being, and I strive daily to embrace this approach to my practice and to make a difference.

REFERENCES

Beabout, B. (2012) 'Turbulence, perturbance, and educational *change*', *Complexity: An International Journal of Complexity and Education*, 9(2): 15–29.

Blanchard, K., Lawrence, M. and Olmstead, C. (2013) *Trust Works! Four Keys to Building Lasting Relationships*. London: HarperCollins.

Brown, B. (2018) *Dare to Lead*. London: Penguin Random House.

Cameron, E. and Green, M. (2012) *Making Sense of Change Management*, 2nd edition. London: Kogan Page.

Dreyfus, H. L. and Dreyfus, S. E. (1986) *Mind over Machine: The Power of Human Intuition and Expertise in the Age of the Computer*. Oxford: Basil Blackwell.

Francke, A. (2019) *Create a Gender-balanced Workplace*. London: Penguin Business Experts.

Hargreaves, A. and O'Connor, M. T. (2018) *Leading Collaborative Professionalism*. Thousand Oaks, CA: Corwin Press.

McKinsey Global Institute (2015) McKinsey&Company. [Online] Available at: https://www.mckinsey.com/~/media/mckinsey/featured%20insights/employment%20and%20growth/how%20advancing%20womens%20equality%20can%20add%2012%20trillion%20to%20global%20growth/mgi%20power%20of%20parity_full%20report_september%202015.pdf (accessed 15 November 2020).

Myatt, M. (2016) *High Challenge, Low Threat: Finding the Balance*. Woodbridge: John Catt Educational.

Thomas-EL, S., Jones, J. M. and Vari, T. J. (2019) *Passionate Leadership: Creating a Culture of Success in Every School*. Thousand Oaks, CA: Corwin Press.

17

OVERCOMING THE *CHALLENGES* OF A WOMAN LEADER WITH A DISABILITY IN EDUCATION

Sharon McCormack

KEY POINTS

This chapter will:

- Explore how I navigated working as a woman in leadership in education with a disability;
- Highlight the negotiation skills I developed;
- Explain the importance of valuing my knowledge, expertise and skills.

I have worked in educational leadership roles over the past 20 years and in education for over 30 years in Melbourne, Australia. I have worked in primary schools mostly and my passion is learning, teaching and working with students and teachers to improve students' educational experiences. I have negotiated and re-negotiated my role as a woman leader over the past 13 years. This is my story and it is one I want to share with you.

INTRODUCTION

The pain was excruciating; I was paralysed by it and any movement amplified the pain. I had collapsed on the floor in the teachers' planning room. I'd felt the build-up of pain; however, I hadn't expected to be completely seized up by it. I heard colleagues call emergency services, the principal arrived to comfort me and, before I knew it, I was heading off to hospital in an ambulance. It wasn't the first time this had happened; I had lost count of the number of trips to hospital I'd had in pain.

I have degenerative disc disease and, since my diagnosis in 2006, I've had four spine operations. The condition means that the discs in my spine are either worn away or prone to prolapse, and I experience ongoing neuropathic (nerve) or musculoskeletal pain. The pain manifests in acute flare-ups or in constant chronic pain. In addition to the physical pain, I have navigated the psychological and social impact this condition has had on me. Ongoing pain heightens emotional responses which, for me, led to depression.

As I headed to the hospital, I had just experienced another acute flare-up. Two weeks in hospital and two weeks in rehabilitation: I had to recover and learn new strategies to manage my condition so that I could return to my life, my family, my work.

A DIFFERENT PATHWAY

Since my diagnosis, I've had to reconsider how I approach my career trajectory in educational leadership. Living with a degenerative disc disease meant that my leadership aspirations had to be put aside whilst I learnt to live with and manage this condition. I had to re-evaluate my identity as an educational leader to find new ways to contribute to education. A woman in leadership faces many barriers; a woman in leadership with a disability faces many more.

The standard career pathway involves moving from being a teacher to a middle leadership role onto an assistant principal role and finally being a principal, and was the pathway I intended to travel; however, after my third successive spine operation across three years, something needed to *change*. After each surgery, I had five weeks of recovery and then the gradual return from part-time to full-time work in my leadership role. While my life had *change*d significantly, I found my workplace remained un*change*d. Sadly, it wasn't flexible in accommodating my needs as expectations and responsibilities remained the same. I negotiated with the principal of the school to step down from my role as Director of Learning and Teaching and take leave without pay. All of this was incredibly daunting – I had huge concerns about my ability to generate an income, but I had to be that 10% braver, I had to believe in myself. My *challenge* was to find a way in which I could continue to share my knowledge and expertise in a different leadership capacity as well as work in a way that accommodated my needs with a disability.

Building the connections to create a network

Networking is incredibly important. I had previously been involved in educational publishing with a major Australian publisher. So, I reached out and contacted the publisher to say I was considering doing more writing and publishing. Interestingly, research shows that men's work and social networks overlap more than do women's networks, and this overlap becomes less and less as women start to have children (Ibarra, 2019). Ibarra (2019) suggests that it is crucial for women to start early and to take a long-term view, ensuring that your network is broad, connective and dynamic. Following up and making the *connection* with the publisher was beneficial as she put me in contact with other publishers and organisations. From 2008, I established my educational consultancy business, *Visible Learning Journeys*, and led and worked on a range of projects with major Australian educational publishers as an educational consultant and author. Developing my own business was exciting, providing opportunities to develop new knowledge and skills, whilst still contributing, albeit in a different way, to learning and teaching across Australian primary school classrooms.

Collaboration can look different in educational leadership

Eventually, I resigned from my position in the primary school as working as an educational consultant offered the opportunity to work from home where I could manage my condition. I experienced a mind shift in developing my business as my *confidence* had increased through taking on a new direction and being 10% braver. In establishing and building a clientele base, I identified and followed up leads by making personal contact with key individuals to develop my professional network, which led to different projects and *collaboration* with a range of professionals. This enabled my business to grow and I am extremely proud of my body of work over this period. Some of the projects that I worked on were shortlisted for the Australian Publishers Association's (APA) Educational Publishing Awards and two of the projects won the Primary Student Resources category in consecutive years.

Developing the confidence to negotiate

Working as an educational consultant and author also meant that I had to negotiate, which was an area in which I had to become 10% braver to earn a living. Negotiations regarding the value I offered meant identifying and discussing my knowledge, expertise and experience, and the scope of the projects. Often, negotiating your own value creates anxiety for women leaders, and it certainly did for me. It is an intimidating conversation as we are often concerned with the perceptions of others: 'The act of professional negotiation has a completely different definition for men than for women' (Sankar, 2017).

In preparing for a negotiation, de Janasz and Cabrera (2018) suggest that it is helpful for women to:

- Identify what you want and know the reason why.
- Consider all the alternatives to the negotiation.
- Develop ways to be persuasive during the negotiation.

Over time, the more practised and confident I became in communicating my value, the better the outcomes. These skills assisted me when I decided to return to school leadership as I was able to *communicate* my value to the school *community*.

RETURNING TO EDUCATIONAL LEADERSHIP IN A SCHOOL COMMUNITY

While I enjoyed developing and working on projects with publishers and collaborating with amazing professionals, writing is solitary work. I missed the day-to-day contact with students and colleagues within a school *community*. However, I could not work full time due to my physical limitations. I found a learning and teaching leadership role for three days a week in a primary school and was delighted to be offered the job after moving through the application process. In accepting the position, I drew on my *communication* and negotiation skills to ensure that this new workplace would meet my physical needs and to consider how the school *community* could support me in my role within the school.

Honest conversations to establish clarity and overcome barriers

Being 10% braver enabled me to negotiate the accommodations and modifications I needed to participate fully in my workplace. You see, my disability is not visible. I must be upfront and open about the daily *challenges* that I face with any prospective employer. It's not always easy to overcome the possible judgements of others regarding whether I am physically capable of maintaining a leadership role. Since my last spine operation in 2014, I have worked hard to manage my condition; I've experienced highs and lows but continue to bounce back from each setback despite the *challenges*. Honest conversations help as I do not want principals to assume what I can do and achieve. Equally, I think many women do assume that others know their value, and we need to be braver in highlighting our value to others. Discussing accommodations and modifications in the workplace with principals is crucial as this provides the *clarity* required when working with a disability. Setting and communicating boundaries are also essential as I know my limitations and my employer must understand them as well. Many schools are not flexible in accommodating the additional needs of teachers, so it's important that I strongly advocate for myself with principals to ensure that the appropriate structures are in place to support my work in schools.

Addressing the challenges as a woman leader with a disability in education

We do need to be 10% braver, as barriers for women in education operate in both overt and covert ways, and to face and address them requires resilience, perseverance, and tenacity. An inner strength is necessary when faced with an unpredictable disability and in challenging systematic barriers. As an educational leader, I've taken a very different journey to the one I anticipated. It has meant continually negotiating and re-negotiating my workplace conditions. In doing so, I can fully access and participate in my role as a woman leader in education. In facing any barrier, I needed to *change* and cultivate a mindset based primarily on my belief in myself to make a difference as an educational leader.

REFLECTING UPON MY EXPERIENCE

My personal and professional journey has brought me here, and I now have the opportunity to contribute in yet another way in education as I have been successful in gaining a scholarship at a leading Australian university to do a PhD . When I reflect upon my professional experience over the past 30 years, I would never have thought that I would consider or have the *confidence* to take on the *challenge* of researching at this level but there are many pathways in educational leadership and being open to different opportunities is both essential and exciting.

Passing on being 10% braver

- Do not undervalue what you bring to your leadership role. As a leader, your knowledge, expertise and experience add value to the experiences of students and colleagues within your school *community*.

- Work on building your professional network. Be intentional and strategic and seek out experiences beyond your school network which offer new professional opportunities.

- Develop and practise your negotiation skills to help you in achieving your career aspirations.

- Open yourself up to new opportunities, and look at all the possibilities and alternatives in developing your career pathway, as there is scope beyond working in schools.

REFERENCES

de Janasz, S. and Cabrera, B. (2018) 'How women can get what they want in a negotiation', *Harvard Business Review*, 17 August [Online]. Available at: https://hbr.org/2018/08/how-women-can-get-what-they-want-in-a-negotiation (accessed 8 December 2019).

Ibarra, H. (2019) 'Why all women need a professional network', *Lean In* [Online]. Available at: https://leanin.org/education/building-effective-networks (accessed 17 December 2019).

Sankar, C. (2017) 'Why don't more women negotiate?', *Forbes*, 13 July [Online]. Available at: www.forbes.com/sites/forbescoachescouncil/2017/07/13/why-dont-more-women-negotiate/#47bd3b03e769 (accessed 17 December 2019).

PART 4
DARING TO BE DIFFERENT

PART

4

18
CAN I SEE YOUR ID?
Gemma Sant Benson

KEY POINTS

This chapter will:

- Show why I needed to be 10% braver as a young leader in education;
- Demonstrate how I owned my achievements, celebrated them and did not let peers undermine my success;
- Explore ways that I counteracted any feelings of imposter syndrome;
- Examine the importance of *communication* and *collaboration*;
- Highlight the importance of talent spotting in others.

INTRODUCTION

Leadership brings with it many *challenges* and, if you are a relatively young leader, then your age can be an additional hurdle to tackle. Competence and craft are not necessarily linked with how many years of experience you have had, and professionals must be valued on their merit and proven abilities. This chapter will look at how to overcome any disadvantage a young leader may face and how to use the role to promote success in an organisation.

UNEXPECTEDLY A HEADTEACHER

At 29, I was acting as the headteacher of a primary school in East London and, after one term, the post was made permanent. This had never been my goal.

I love teaching because it presents a daily opportunity to inspire and ignite a passion for discovery. This was what attracted me to the profession after finishing my psychology degree – I was the first in my family to attend university. I had never really considered where this career might take me but I have a good work ethic and see each new opportunity as a learning experience.

Much like #WomenEd, I see *challenge* as hugely positive and something to be celebrated, and I have a rather more archetypal masculine approach: say yes and think about it later. As a result of this attitude, I had started my Masters in Education whilst still an NQT and took on the role of subject lead for Geography in a primary school, even though I could not navigate my way to the end of my street. A few years later, I joined the leadership team of a failing school in East London as an assistant head-teacher and then became headteacher. We took the school from special measures to outstanding and I was still only in my 20s. My success came from my work ethic and a keen interest in effective leadership. Did I feel worried that I was not ready for each new stage of my career? Of course, but I did not let self-doubt and the fear of success slow me down.

I wanted to make the most of every opportunity that I could, something that was really driven by my enjoyment of learning and developing. In an interview, David Bowie (2016) provided a marvellous mix of motivation and reassurance: you are not work-ing in the right area if you feel too safe. He said that you should walk just out of your depth until your feet are just off of the bottom; that is the right place to do something exciting. This is a message I often tell myself whenever I feel too comfortable at work and when I go after an opportunity that makes me nervous; that is when I know that I am in the right place for something exciting and new to happen.

OVERCOMING IMPOSTER SYNDROME

Challenge to my position came from older teachers: 'I've been teaching since before you were a dot in your mother's tummy' and 'so what makes you so special that you have got to where you are at such a young age?' are examples of the comments that I have faced during my leadership career. When you are already unsure about how worthy you are, it is only made worse when people put a voice to your worries. Whilst I have never suffered from crippling imposter syndrome, I have had moments where I have had a crisis of *confidence* and I noticed that they became more frequent with each promotion.

Researchers have associated imposter syndrome with highly effective, highly suc-cessful people and it is often linked to those who can be described as perfectionists, particularly women (Cox, 2018). Knowing this and understanding that we are not alone when we experience self-doubt or worry that we are not keeping up with other people in similar positions means that we do not have to fall victim to imposter syndrome and that we can, maybe, even use it to our advantage.

Corkindale (2008) highlights the importance of recognising these feelings as you experience them. Is there any pattern or trend to how they are triggered? Being mind-ful of these apparently negative emotions is important because if you acknowledge their presence then it can help you to dissociate from them and, in my experience, limit their influence on thought processes. The messages that we tell ourselves have enormous impact. When feelings of inadequacy plague us, recognise them and then remind yourself that there is no way to know everything and that feeling out of your comfort zone means that you are learning; it is your knowledge, openmindedness to develop and skill that earned you your position. This is a powerful mechanism to develop and, for me at least, it is a conscious thought process that I steer myself to when feelings of imposter syndrome creep in.

I often analyse my own internal messages and the effect that they have on how I feel about myself and what I am doing. Caring about my job and the people that I work with means that any form of self-sabotage is damaging, not only to myself, but also to those to whom I am accountable and responsible for. It is really helpful to imagine that, rather than talking to yourself, you are speaking to a loved one. Are the messages that you tell yourself as kind as those that you would say to someone that you really care about? Is this what you would want someone to say to your child or partner?

The #WomenEd values are a great tool to guide anyone through career progression because they *challenge* people to be at least 10% braver. *Challenge* and *change* often mean a new opportunity, but there is a suggested gender difference in how people respond to this set of circumstances, and I find that this can also apply to age. Research by Kay and Shipman (2014) shows that men will approach a situation, role or opportunity for which they are underqualified and underprepared with *confidence* and gusto. On the other hand, women who are overqualified and over-prepared (although the perfectionist in me says that it is impossible to be over-prepared – always battling that inner doubting voice) will still hold back from situations. This research, though focused on gender, resonated with me as a young leader. The older candidates applying for the same job role as me seemed to take *confidence* from competing with a younger person for a position, assuming that I could not possibly be as suitable as they were, despite the fact that my experience and success may have outweighed theirs. My initial reaction to their misplaced reassurance that they were the better candidate based on their age was to feel intimidated and inferior, but I fought against this and *change*d the messages that I told myself. Waiting to interview, I would think through my successes and achievements to ensure that I was building my own *confidence* rather than sabotaging myself with self-doubt. I reminded myself of the determination, grit and ability that got me to where I am. I was not going to be prevented from fulfilling my potential simply because I was conforming to simplistic expectations of how a younger person should steer their career or how competent they may be compared to someone older. So let's use our inner critic to our advantage, for it is that internal voice that keeps us striving and setting high expectations. But as soon as we feel it limiting our accomplishments, we should simply acknowledge it and then ignore it. It just takes being 10% braver.

DEMONSTRATING COMPETENCE

As a young leader, it sometimes feels unjust to have to face *challenge* or scepticism from people that I cannot fulfil my role based on how many years I have been alive. It would make me feel uncomfortable when people *change*d the way that they spoke to me once they found out that I was a headteacher, or would express their own embarrassment when they made an incorrect assumption about my position at work based on my age. To deal with this *challenge* is not easy, but here I was and I needed to make some decisions.

So, I cut my hair and bought blazers. It seems futile now and rather shallow but I wanted to convey the look of a trustworthy, intellectual leader and thought that shorter hair and a serious-looking blazer would serve me better than longer locks; an expectation of age and appearance that I was distracted by. I was trying to fit into a mould of what a school leader might look like and, with people doubtful of my capability based on my age, I tried to convey readiness and ability in a superficial way to counteract that. What I came to learn though is that confident *communication* is really what matters, along with feeling confident in how you present yourself as a professional. *Communication* as a young leader requires you to be 10% braver. It is about expressing yourself in a way that reassures people that you know what you are doing and, sometimes, perception is just as important as reality.

Research by Zenger and Folkman (2015) found that younger leaders are less likely to be trusted by older colleagues, and I accepted that I would need to work harder at earning their trust and respect, but it was not easy. I did this, broadly, in two ways. I demonstrated my *confidence* through the sharing of initiatives and ideas (Glickman, 2011) and I orchestrated teamwork of which I was also a part. Engaging with people and actively seeking out feedback is a powerful strategy. As Nelson (2012) says, 'people want to be considered, to belong and to contribute'. The proportion of staff who are engaged in their job more than doubles once they are working as part of a team (Buckingham and Goodall, 2019). During this collaborative working, attitudes and opinions from older peers who had 'seen it all before' could be patronising and undermining. Whilst I was very conscious of communicating with these staff members in a way that respected their experience, knowledge and feelings, this was not always reciprocated. I find that people sometimes make assumptions about the type of person I am based on being young and successful: I must be hardened and tough. It takes me being 10% braver to build positive relationships with colleagues who can underestimate the emotional effect of devaluing my capabilities based on my younger age.

Through teamwork, you are collaborating to connect and support just as #WomenEd describes it. Age becomes insignificant as you all come together as one group. Once people can see your skill set in action and that you actively seek to work as part of the collective, you are proving your competence. Behaviour is *communication* and seeing is believing. I embrace opportunities to show people that I deserve to be in the role that I have, just as colleagues demonstrate this to me; as members of a team, we are all accountable to each other and this should not be a top-down phenomenon.

GIVING YOUR POWER AND INFLUENCE AWAY

Empowering others is incredibly important for the sustained long-term success of an organisation, and making it meaningful, long-lasting and authentic requires sharing leadership and influence. This is a higher-order skill: to be able to do something yourself to a competent level is one thing, but to be able to mentor someone else to do it as well as you, if not better, takes an even greater level of skill and capability. This is not to be linked to years of experience.

I needed to be brave enough to mentor fellow leaders and potential leaders to be great at their job. This is something that I did with success, and now my former deputy and assistant headteachers have progressed to headship. Providing others with the space and opportunity to thrive is another way that I demonstrate my ability as a successful leader. Now, at 32 years old, I am developing and flexing new skills as I assume my new position as executive headteacher within a group of schools. This will bring a new set of *challenge*s and presumptions based on my age that will need me to be 10% braver to adapt to them. But remember, every *challenge* is an opportunity.

Passing on being 10% braver

- Use your inner critic to your advantage; do not let it undermine your hard work and success. If the doubting voice makes you feel insecure about your achievements, then stop listening to it.

- Be kind to yourself - speak to yourself as you would a loved one.

- Know that you will need to prove your competency and be ready to do so as part of a team. Being younger in age means that you may have to work harder to prove yourself, but it is worth doing.

- Winning and being the best at whatever you do means that you are not learning or growing. Allow yourself to be in positions where you are not the expert - it is the only way you learn.

- Use your position to talent-spot and develop others to be successful in their own right. Do not let your age put you off doing this with colleagues who may be older than you.

REFERENCES

Bowie, D. (2016) 'David Bowie explains why you should go a little further', interview by *Goalcast*, 10 January. Available at: www.goalcast.com/2016/01/10/david-bowie-explains-why-you-should-go-a-little-further-video (accessed 11 July 2020).

Buckingham, M. and Goodall, A. (2019) 'The power of hidden teams', *Harvard Business Review*, 20 May [Online]. Available at: https://hbr.org/cover-story/2019/05/the-power-of-hidden-teams (accessed 26 August 2019).

Corkindale, G. (2008) 'Overcoming imposter syndrome', *Harvard Business Review*, 7 May [Online]. Available at: https://hbr.org/2008/05/overcoming-imposter-syndrome (accessed 26 October 2019).

Cox, E. (2018) 'What is imposter syndrome and how can you combat it?', *Ted Talk*, August [Online]. Available at: www.ted.com/talks/elizabeth_cox_what_is_imposter_syndrome_and_how_can_you_combat_it?language=en#t-125225 (accessed 27 August 2019).

Glickman, J. (2011) 'Leading older employees', *Harvard Business Review*, 5 April [Online]. Available at: https://hbr.org/2011/04/leading-older-employees (accessed 23 August 2019).

Kay, K. and Shipman, C. (2014) *The Confidence Code*. New York: HarperCollins.

Nelson, A. (2012) 'How women lead differently, and why it matters', *Fast Company*, 9 August. Available at: www.fastcompany.com/3000249/how-women-lead-differently-and-why-it-matters (accessed 11 July 2020).

Zenger, J. and Folkman, J. (2015) 'What younger managers should know about how they're perceived', *Harvard Business Review*, 29 September [Online]. Available at: https://hbr.org/2015/09/what-younger-managers-should-know-about-how-theyre-perceived (accessed 22 August 2019).

19

WHY IT'S 'IN' TO BE AN INTROVERTED LEADER

Alex Fairlamb

KEY POINTS

Why I had to be 10% braver:

- I was promoted to a new position as a member of the senior leadership team (SLT);
- I began to work with and promote Girl-Kind, an organisation which empowers girls to *challenge* the media stereotypes of girls as well as discuss the *challenge*s they face as girls living in the north-east;
- I needed to *challenge* concerns about the lack of diversity within the history national curriculum.

INTRODUCTION

'How can you claim to be an introvert if you're a leader?' is a comment which is often said to me when I describe my character traits, a reaction which suggest that the words introvert and leader are an oxymoron and that the two cannot be symbiotic. It is often interpreted (thus an unconscious bias) that being an introvert means that you are perhaps reserved, quiet, closed off and don't contribute to as many conversations as others.

Yet, here I find myself; a proud introvert who is leading in different areas of my history and SLT career. My 10% braver moment came when I realised I could *challenge* diversity leadership issues through Girl-Kind, a gender network within the trust of schools, and a country-wide battle cry to develop diversity within our history curriculum. I tapped into my skills of research and my ability to assess what avenues of action would enable my voice to be heard most effectively, without adopting a faux-extravert personality to do so. So, I say, let's *challenge* and shake up these negative introvert connotations, dispel the myths and reclaim it as a leadership strength.

AN INTROVERTED LEADER? WHAT STEREOTYPES DOES THIS EVOKE?

It concerns me that if you research the term 'introvert' you'll be met with three types of article:

1. How to use your introvert nature as a strength, highlighting that many are facing an unconscious bias or criticism.

2. Introvert versus extravert quizzes (Psychologies, 2018) – putting aside the accuracy of taking such quizzes, at what point did it become a 'versus' mentality, pitching the traits against one another in such a binary, either/or and good-versus-bad duel? (No, 2019)

And, more worryingly:

3. How to overcome your inner introvert (a danger highlighted by Kahnweiler, 2013), an affliction in need of curing, in that being gregarious is the key to effective leadership.

The time has come to claim the characteristic back and celebrate the many gifts (Ronson, 2012) of introvert characteristics, in the vein of Buelow's (2015) 'superpower' stance: reflective, active listeners who are observational and take the time to assess situations and articulate ideas; leaders who are continuous learners.

THE CHALLENGES I FACED AS A SENIOR LEADER

My rapid promotion to the senior leadership team (SLT) meant that I was immersed in situations such as meetings where school priorities are discussed, *challenges* are raised and actions are determined. Having previously been a lead practitioner (a teacher with leadership responsibility), I had some experience of leadership but it was within my own field of expertise – history and teaching and learning; this was my comfort zone. I spent two months disorientated; I was in an environment of rapid-fire questions, demands for opinions and the expectation to propose different initiatives. This came in tandem with facing probing questions about those proposals, which I had to be prepared to answer on the spot, with knowledge and *confidence*, such as written academic reports. This requirement to respond immediately played against my traits of being a deep thinker, diplomatic and cautious; someone who likes to reflect before responding. As a creative person, the proposals I put forward were appropriately *challenged* as it would require culture *changes* in areas of the school. I was an introvert out of water and feared looking like I was incompetent as a result.

September came and it was time for the annual Girl-Kind project to begin. Girl-Kind asks the young girls involved, 'What are the *challenges* and opportunities of growing up as a girl in the North East?' (Girl-Kind, 2019) and through project work they then stage interventions on the UN Day of the Girl. I am privileged to work with these young women during this time and I witness a range of them use their voice to *challenge* multiple barriers, irrespective of their interests, backgrounds and personalities – including those who are introverted. The ethos of the project and the bravery of the girls inspired me to evolve as a leader, and therefore use my introvert traits as strengths to support a collective agenda of *change*, including challenging stereotypes – introversion being one of them.

As I saw the girls flourish in this challenging environment, one where they bare all about the issues they face, I realised that each had a unique nature and there was a sense of strength and beauty in the way that they articulated what they were saying, in their very different ways. Thank goodness I did, because Hollywood films and the media would have had me believe that as an introvert I was only ever going to be seen as difficult (Katniss, *The Hunger Games*), as strange (Violet, *The Incredibles*) or as the socially awkward leper (*Amelie*) that no one wants to interact with and rolls their eyes when they see them enter a room. I took time to reflect on this and serendipitously I came across #WomenEd on Twitter, a supportive *community* which promotes *confidence* and *connections*.

I returned to the SLT table with a new perspective and an energy rooted in the *confidence* that, actually, my introvert traits were my strength. I used to be worried that after discussions had concluded, I would suddenly request to revisit the last item as I had thought of something. My old mindset would tell me that I looked like I was being too slow to know what was happening. My new mindset now tells me: 'I'm reflective. I listen and consider things through internal processing, I consider perspectives and make sense of things, and I form ideas carefully in order to talk meaningfully.' It's not that I'm being slow, it's that my mind is working through the different possibilities, searching for the research knowledge I may have about the issue, and evaluating what could be a possible course through this. I've become more vocal in discussions, doing so at a measured pace. I now say, 'I'd like to do some research on this and then revisit it, so that we have an evidence base.' I celebrate my research geekery and use it to positively contribute to meetings and to *challenge*, rather than worry that it makes me appear awkward or negative. It makes me a stronger member of the team, and complements the differing traits of the SLT who think quickly or *challenge* more directly.

I have lost the fear that my introversion may mean that I look at things in creative ways that differ from others. It doesn't mean that I'm wrong or lacking in ability as I've gone in a different direction from the norm. It means that I can bring a different perspective, and, when used with my research skills, I can present alternative solutions. They may not always be right, but at least I've highlighted a different way of looking at the issue. This has meant more rapid-fire, challenging questions to justify my ideas, which plays against my strength of thinking before I speak, but my belief and my assurance in the preparation that I have done and my strong sense of self have emboldened me.

THE CHALLENGE AS A HISTORY TEACHER

When I became a history teacher, I was concerned about the lack of diversity within the national curriculum (gender, culture and ethnicity). I didn't know if I, as an introvert, could be the one to *challenge* this. My concern is that often there is a tokenistic approach to teaching women's history. Selected narratives reinforce student perceptions that women of the past are:

1. Marginally significant, given their absence from key points studied or the 'bolt on' feature of women towards the end of the topic.
2. Hysterical and emotionally impotent beings with no agency, aside from Elizabeth I, until the emergence of the Suffragettes, second-wave bra burners and Thatcher (as a northerner, you can imagine my feelings about that!)

Then I joined and became the coordinator of TMHistoryIcons (a national history teachmeet). I now work with my amazing 'history family' who have encouraged me to use my introvert skills to champion the right things to do for the *community* to drive practice forward. This has included my recent battle cry of 'bra burners, banshees and battle-axes', a talk about the need to have a 'blended, not binary' approach to teaching history and one that avoids a narrow-lens approach to teaching women's history. And, yes, it features introverted women, such as Eleanor Roosevelt and Rosa Parks. Rosa Parks was herself an introvert: her 1994 book *Quiet Strength* highlights this. Whilst said to be timid, her leadership legacy of non-violent civil disobediance has had significant impact and she inspired millions. Her protest could have taken a very different tone or form. However, her observations of Gandhi and her reflection on the nature of American attitudes and the judicial system meant that she sagaciously *challenge*d the National Association for the Advancement of Colored People's decision on action, deploying methods of protest which played to her strengths (Simkin, 1997).

N-GENDER

As a result of working with Girl-Kind and TMHistoryIcons, I set up a gender network across the trust of schools that I work within. I used research to highlight the need for it and to write a structured argument, making reference to #WomenEd and gender networks elsewhere. I received a swift email of support and approval from my executive headteacher which was very heartening. With the lack of positively portrayed introvert role models in our culture, I feel that my honesty about my introversion will be what I can bring to this network. It's a myth that introverts are unsociable and can't connect with people. We connect in different ways. We form strong friendships or professional bonds with people that are lasting and based on shared areas of interest or expertise. It's not the quantity of people we network with, but the meaningful quality of the relationships that we have and that we nurture over time.

I can't say that everyone has been converted to seeing my introvert ways as a positive characteristic. Someone suggested that the new network was 'for emos you knew at school, who now attention seek in other ways', but that has simply reinforced the need for such a network and why the noun of introvert needs reclaiming. (And, yes, I was an emo in high school. So what?) That's why I proudly wear an 'Introvert Girl Gang' t-shirt!

Passing on being 10% braver

- Play to your introvert strengths of considered argument. Use and maximise your introvert strengths. Be more Rosa - research then roar!

- Reflection as a strength - your skills of research mean that you are invaluable as a leader. Be confident in saying: 'we need to reflect on this and revisit it/carry out research first.'

- In a team, you are an asset, an important piece of the jigsaw. You complement the extrovert, you bring a different perspective and process to considering things, you are a calming influence and you have creative solutions. Be confident in this, don't compare with others and instead celebrate and use those skills.

- Meaningful *connections* - cherish and cultivate the *connections* you have, and don't measure them by the *amount* of *connections* you have.

REFERENCES

Buelow, B. (2015) *The Introvert Entrepreneur: Amplify Your Strengths and Create Success on Your Own Terms.* New York: TarcherPerigee.

Girl-Kind (2019) Homepage. [Online]. Available at: www.girlkind.co.uk (accessed 25 October 2019).

Kahnweiler, J. B. (2013) *The Introverted Leader: Building on Your Quiet Strength.* San Francisco, CA: Berrett-Koehler.

No, M. (2019) This Test Will Determine What % Social Introvert You Are [Online]. Available at: www.buzzfeed.com/michelleno/percent-social-introvert-quiz (accessed 5 August 2019).

Parks, R., with Reed, G. J. (1994) *Quiet Strength.* Grand Rapids, MI: Zondervan.

Psychologies (2018) Test: Are you an Introvert or an Extrovert? [Online]. Available at: www.psychologies.co.uk/self/are-you-an-introvert-or-an-extrovert.html (accessed 5 August 2019).

Ronson, J. (2012) 'Quiet: The power of introverts in a world that can't stop talking by Susan Cain – Review', *The Guardian*, 22 March [Online]. Available at: www.theguardian.com/books/2012/mar/22/quiet-power-introverts-susan-cain-review (accessed 5 August 2019).

Simkin, J. (1997) Rosa Parks [Online]. Available at: https://spartacus-educational.com/USAparksR.htm (accessed 5 August 2019).

20
DISORGANISED LEADERSHIP
Jules Daulby

KEY POINTS

This chapter will:

- Describe my life as a neurodiverse leader;
- Explore how I am myself within the context of my life circumstances;
- Encourage you too to be 10% braver by showing vulnerability;
- Advocate for leading with kindness.

INTRODUCTION

I didn't know I had ADHD. I was always told at school that I could do better, that I was disruptive and that I was clever but was wasting it. I had messy handwriting which didn't help and, even now, it makes me feel nauseous if I write for too long. The laptop is my friend and this would have completely *change*d my exam grades had I been able to type. I was also impulsive which meant I constantly blurted things out in class (I still do in meetings and can dominate them; I've learned to metaphorically put a hand over my mouth). I will also be the one who gets up to make tea or go to the toilet in a meeting; I can't stay still for too long.

ABOUT ME

I was bad at maths. I now know that I can do higher-order maths but I need a lot longer than most and I can't memorise times tables. Ordering the alphabet is also not automatic. These skills are linked to short-term memory, of which I have a limited capacity in comparison to my peers. I'm good at talking but not necessarily sequencing my thoughts and, whilst I can write, it's effortful and a bit clunky. The longer the word count, the harder it gets; 500 yep, 1,000 erm, 10,000 what?!

I'm a procrastinator and a day dreamer. I can have mood swings and will often lose my temper in the house with my kids or my partner when we're rushing and busy. I get easily overwhelmed if I have too much to do and can end up doing nothing. It's very much dependent on how I feel; sometimes I'm incredibly efficient and can work faster than anyone I know, but I can't sustain it. I'm messy and disorganised but have moments when I pull it all together really quickly; again it depends on the feels. Although I often struggle to maintain focus, I can hyper-focus. This is an ADHD trait which is less known than attention deficit. It means that once a person finds something they're interested in, it is very difficult to transition to something else. For our learners, it means difficulty moving between subjects and is why you may hear teachers saying 'they were able to do it yesterday'. For an adult, it can mean neglecting other areas of life whilst they are in hyper-focused mode, and it can be frustrating for colleagues waiting for a task to be completed and seeing the person concentrating on something which is of less urgency. Where often for those with ADHD they hear and notice everything which means it can be hard to concentrate, once hyper-focused, the house could be burning down and they might not notice.

I've walked out of a number of jobs and left many relationships on impulse after a perceived injustice. I never go back and struggle to forgive. I thought this stuff was normal and it wasn't until I began specialist teaching in dyslexia and learning about other special needs that I realised that it wasn't; that whilst I had great strengths which masked problematic areas, I have special educational needs.

THE GOOD NEWS

But let me tell you of my strengths: I am a risk taker, creative and energetic. I have a mind which sees and understands things others don't, yet may miss the completely obvious. I am often described by friends as the cleverest person they know but also the stupidest. I take on every project offered (this is not always sensible) and defend the underdogs. I can unwisely sacrifice my own comfort and money for others, a source of great contention in my house because I'm also responsible for paying the bills. My partner and four children would like to see that money and spend time with me.

I have good friends and a partner I've been with for nearly 30 years; I am loyal – once you are a friend, I would die for you (well, maybe not die, but you get what I mean). I have never struggled getting work, do well in interviews, can make a difference quickly wherever I work and I pick things up fast. I know that I'm exciting to work with, people gain *confidence* with me and my energy is contagious. One of my old friends said that no matter what chaos was happening in school, when I walked through the door she knew everything would be all right. It was a lovely thing to hear.

So, let's mix those strengths and weaknesses up. I'm exhausting and can cause chaos but, with the right team, can make radical *change*. What is important is to have people to balance me out – where I can start a project, I do not necessarily pay attention to detail so I work well with people who are very organised and question my ideas and think through how an idea can work in practice. There's also something about finishing a project which I am less skilled at, and I like working with those who are good at finishing something which I started with great enthusiasm but then became focused on the next project.

I rely on scaffolding, mainly from other people. I need help with organisation, administration and focus. This is not because I'm too important to do admin, I'm just really bad at it. I still don't know how to create a group email and I take ages completing tasks that take others a few minutes. I depend on getting on well with people and feeling comfortable. I used to try to hide my memory difficulties but now I'm very honest about them and have found there is a difference between apologising for being me and explaining why my difficulties are there.

#WOMENED

When I met my fellow co-founders (Keziah, Natalie, Sameena, Hannah, Helena and Vivienne) of #WomenEd, I was a bit bowled over; I have imposter syndrome and still wonder if they believe I'm someone more intelligent, more capable and generally a better person than I really am. They persist in including me, however ... now I'm wondering if it's out of charity?

#WomenEd is bittersweet for me. I am exposed to the most incredible women leaders but I feel like a little girl who knows nothing and can do nothing. Walking on the shoulders of giants feels very appropriate; was it a joke when Vivienne asked me to join the steering group? Did she confuse me with someone else? I often look over my shoulder when people compliment me to see who they're talking to.

And this is how life is for a woman with ADHD, I think: feeling wracked with self-doubt, often considered an underachiever, with glimpses of brilliance but bucket loads of cock-ups, and sees the best in people but the worst in themselves. #WomenEd helps me *challenge* this narrative. What am I good at? Well, I can stand up and speak to large crowds, I am happy to debate education with anyone, no matter how important they are, and I know my onions regarding SEND (I have finally realised that). I've been in it long enough and have taught long enough to feel confident to say that I am a specialist in literacy and inclusion. That's not to say I have nothing left to learn – quite the opposite – but I am good at what I do and have a voice which is worth hearing.

WHEN ADHD BECAME A BURDEN RATHER THAN A SUPERPOWER

It was not until a few years ago that my ADHD started to become something which seemed to be hindering rather than helping. This was linked to various *challenge*s happening in my life. I'd fallen out with the charity where I was director of education at the same time as two significant family crises were occurring and, to top it all off, I was going through the menopause. The combination was toxic and led to a point where I had no job, no money and my career prospects looked dire. As well as feeling constantly anxious and overwhelmed, my working memory seemed worse than ever and I couldn't concentrate on anything for long. All my weaknesses had come to the fore and my strengths were further hidden.

The #WomenEd *community* remained relevant and supported me through this difficult time. I chose to try being a freelancer and there were many women I spoke to about this. I was offered work, writing and public speaking opportunities and I was surviving quite nicely. However, I missed being part of a team and teaching. It was after meeting an old boss for coffee that I began teaching again. Eventually, I ended up working at her school and becoming head of *communication*. I couldn't believe how content I felt; teaching was my safe space. Being in the classroom with the students was my comfort zone and designing a new English curriculum was a prospect I relished. The job was challenging enough without being too stressful. I'd been very honest at my interview, about falling out with the charity and my circumstances, and it felt liberating to show vulnerability without feeling judged. The job was fun and I was beginning to feel myself again. #WomenEd helped me see that choosing what is right for you is a vital part of career development.

With my family situation, my mental health and stage of life, I was cautious in thinking about promotion as my current post may have been the perfect leadership position, giving me the flexibility to do a small amount of public speaking and training independently, write my books and remain authentic as a teacher and a middle leader. With the support of #WomenEd I was 10% braver and am now a senior leader again. And #WomenEd will not judge me; not all leadership journeys are a straight line – they can zig zag, especially for someone with ADHD. It is for individuals to choose what's right for them – don't underestimate yourself but also decide truthfully where you want to be. This may not be the final destination on my journey, but I've unpacked as I think I'm going to spend a long time here. I feel settled and safe.

Passing on being 10% braver

- Use your strengths and find scaffolding for things which are not within your skill set.

- Be kind - people react to stress, *change* and *challenge* in various ways: always uphold the Nolan Principles (see www.gov.uk/government/publications/the-7-principles-of-public-life).

- Recognise people's circumstances. Length of service isn't necessarily the guide. For example, someone who has been in the job for 15 years may still have times when they are not working to their full capability, so be kind and patient. Similarly, with new teachers who are keen to take on everything, protect them from burnout.

- Choose what's right for you in your leadership journey. It's OK to take your time but, equally, some of you are ready much earlier. Be ambitious but be you.

21
WALKING GAILY FORWARD
Lisa Hannay

KEY POINTS

This chapter will:

- Explore why, to lead fully and wholly, I must be true to my identity as a lesbian woman;
- Show why, to be open to growing and evolving, I must live in truth;
- Show how, to be an example to others, I need to embrace the #WomenEd 8 Cs; particularly for me, *connection, community* and *challenge*.

INTRODUCTION

Fear, secrets and shame do not allow people to grow. Parker J. Palmer in his book *Courage to Teach* (1998) talks about the inner landscape of the teacher. The condition of our inner landscape impacts how we project who we are, what we know, and our very soul to those around us. If my inner landscape is sown with fear, shame and secrets, I can only mirror this in my interactions and in my work. To evolve as a woman and develop as a leader, I have learned that sharing my story is a powerful tool. Living in truth draws people closer, whilst hiding in the dark pushes people away. One person who lives in truth can also inspire others to do the same. In a school, where leaders live and tell their personal narratives and embrace vulnerability, creativity flourishes and *community* develops. It has become particularly important to me to share my identity as a lesbian woman; as I advocate for others to live their truths, I must live mine.

BECOMING

I have often felt, and occasionally still feel, as if I am on the outside looking in, and I think this is because I have been holding back. Before I came out as a lesbian, I know this feeling of isolation was because I was holding a secret coloured with shame and felt that I didn't have the courage to invest fully. I have always been committed to my work and driven to succeed, and through the years began realising that the good, deep work I wanted to engage in had to be sown in truth. Secrets and shame are pervasive and stop us short from being fully present. Brene Brown, in *Dare to Lead* (Brown, 2018: 119), describes shame as the 'never good enough' emotion. If we feel 'not good enough' in one area of our lives, this feeling can quickly engulf our whole being. We need to be, I need to be, truthful in order to evolve fully as an effective leader.

EARLY DAYS

I came out quite late as a lesbian. I simply didn't have the language, experiences and certainly not the exposure growing up to understand or to know that there were such things as lesbians. Growing up in a heteronormative home, I had assumed the role of straight girl who would meet a boy, date, get married and live happily ever after. Today, young people see gay people on television, have access to gay characters in books, have role models, education and, of course, social media that can both enlighten and confuse. Young people today also live in a more accepting world, although there is great room for improvement. There was little room for being different when I was growing up.

I remember when a physician first asked me, 'Which way do you swing?' I was utterly perplexed. I asked for clarification and, upon receiving it, felt instant calm. Of course, that was it. I had never felt an attraction to men, had never had a relationship and the concept of dating, marrying and having children was entirely foreign to me. I did not live in that calm place for long. Fear and shame took root in my heart and soul and it took a few more years of struggle until I finally accepted and began living as a lesbian woman. Struggle is a necessary part of life, but shame is not. When we decide to enter the arena without our armour, we connect with others, *challenge* the status quo and *change* perceptions.

OUT AT WORK

The first person I told was a colleague at work. New in recovery and attending Alcoholics Anonymous, I was learning that living in lies could lead to slips. My biggest secret was that I was a lesbian and this secret was also one of the reasons I drank for so long. I did not want to drink any longer and needed to be honest about my sexual orientation, even if it came at a cost. It was frightening saying the words: 'I am gay.' Upon reflection, no one I have ever come out to has been particularly shocked or surprised. Many have said; 'Of course you are. I knew that', or 'Yes, I was just waiting for you to tell me'. Coming out in rural Alberta, Canada, well anywhere really, but in a conservative area, being different almost always comes with a cost and I had heard terrible stories of other gay people being victimised, harassed and assaulted for living openly. I was not yet brave enough to live fully and openly in this rural setting so I made a move to Calgary.

CONFIDENCE

My identity is largely wrapped up in my role as an educator and thus it became increasingly important to be out at the different schools at which I worked. This is no easy undertaking and leads directly into my first piece of advice: no one can dictate or direct anyone else's coming out. There is indeed great pressure to be out and to this day I don't always disclose my orientation.

Every summer whilst on holiday there is someone who inevitably remarks that I could find a man to travel with or find my 'knight in shining armour' whilst strolling through European castles. I have never corrected nor educated these people, perhaps because of a lingering fear of being 'not good enough' or because I am still not certain, nor perhaps believe it my responsibility to disrupt their personal narratives about gender or sexuality. This realisation leads to my second piece of advice: you do not need to tell everyone your sexual orientation. This identity belongs to you and you alone. There is a difference between keeping a secret and being private. One of the values or 8 Cs of #WomenEd is *confidence*. Coming out has consequences and every person thinking of coming out must think through all the possibilities. *Confidence* does not come all at once. If 10% braver seems like 100%, scale it back. Start with 1%!

ADVOCATING IN SCHOOL

I do believe that in my work life, particularly with students and other staff, people need to see a range of personalities, even amongst LGBTQ+ people. My third piece of advice: we get to advocate for equality in our own way. Parades aren't for everyone. I live a quiet existence and my sexual orientation is simply one part of who I am. At every school I have worked since coming out, I have become braver in each location, coming out to more and more staff and students and living fully as a lesbian woman.

Sometimes we are the closest example of a gay person people meet and we can disarm the perceptions they have formulated about gay people. In many instances, coming out at school has made me the safe place to land for people who have questions, who need to ask for help in navigating the ever-evolving language within the gender and sexually diverse *community*. Another value of #WomenEd is *challenge* and, by being out at work and being a safe harbour for others, I can contribute in a small way to building a foundation for inclusivity. An act as simple as putting a rainbow sticker on my office door sends a loud message, particularly when my colleagues also apply stickers to their doors.

CLARITY

Here is the thing about coming out: we come out all the time, with every new job and potentially every new person we meet. There was that pivotal first time of acknowledging for myself that I was a lesbian and that angst-ridden first time of telling that first person, but, for me, to continue living truthfully, if the situation calls for it, I let people know that I am a lesbian. I need to keep challenging those around me to be inclusive. A result of always having to tell our story is that we face our truth constantly. For me, just as secrets beget secrets, truths beget truths. Telling my truth about my alcoholism led to my truth about my orientation. Being brave each time I tell someone that I am a lesbian builds emotional capital and resolve. I grow stronger each time I tap into being vulnerable.

To quote Oprah: 'What I know for sure is that speaking your truth is the most powerful tool we have' (Female Lead, accessed from Twitter, 28 September 2019).

This clarity around my identity and living my truth has impacted my leadership, making me more vulnerable, approachable and open to learning. Brene Brown, in *Dare to Lead* (2018: 43), writes: 'Vulnerability is the cornerstone of courage-building' and 'without courage there is no creativity or innovation'. Innovation, creativity, risk taking and *collaboration* are all qualities of a great leader and all require us to be vulnerable. There are increasing complexities in every school and teams need to take on more than ever before. Teams need to devise new strategies and manage teaching and learning in ways that they didn't before; they need to lean in and be vulnerable with one another to build success in their schools.

CONNECTION

Always a thinker and always outspoken, I had been ruminating on my truths and determining who I was as a leader when I attended a conference where several #WomenEd *change* makers were presenting and where @WomenEdCanada was conceived. It was at this conference that I started weaving together the power of being out and the power of narrative and truth telling and the impact this awareness had on my leadership. It was at this conference and in the time that has elapsed since that I have realised fully what I had always known on some level, but had never tapped into: being braver, even 10% braver, and living intentionally makes me a better leader. When we are brave about who we are, we take risks in our development as leaders, we feel more confident to reach out and network with others who desire to do likewise.

COMMUNITY

The messages I give myself are often still rooted in 'not good enough'. I tell myself, and joke frequently, that I am not a people person, that I don't care for, nor am good at, networking, and that I am much better working in the background by myself. These messages are lies, cover-ups, remnants from a time when shame was the chest plate in my armour. Teamwork is personal and our personal lives intertwine with our professional lives. I live in a straight world. Even in professional conversations, people talk about their families, their kids, what they did on their summer holidays or weekends with their families and kids. Before coming out at work, these conversations were difficult, and I always found myself holding back, talking in code and avoiding pronouns when talking about anyone in my personal life. This subterfuge creates walls in teams.

Our narratives are most powerful when lived as a whole story, rather than as a chapter in a book, and we build a strong school *community* when everyone can see themselves in the work and everyone is included for where they are in their personal journey. I feel a deep sense of belonging at school and with my colleagues. The collegiality is restorative and liberating as it is based on mutual respect and acceptance, and is where we draw upon our differences and uniqueness to forward the important work of teaching and learning.

CREATING CHANGE

I maintain that being out at work is a personal choice and that no one can dictate the how, why and when of this momentous decision. However, I have come to a slow realisation that when I stand up and live with intention and truth, others might also do the same. A popular quote on social media, 'Empowered people empower others', is only true if people are brave enough, are courageous enough to be who they are and, as in my case, are out at work. Status quo is only *challenge*d when I am brave enough to create *change*.

Passing on being 10% braver

Living divided and in pieces, compartmentalising who I am, no longer works for me as a woman and as a leader. I have chosen to live 'with an unarmored heart' (Brown, 2018: 72). Living with 'wholeheartedness' means 'engaging in our lives from a place of worthiness' (2018: 72). Letting go of fear and shame has unburdened my soul and I have been able to embrace my worth as a woman and as a leader, lesbian and all. If you are thinking of coming out, my suggestions would be the following:

- Find one trusted colleague and tell them first. Practise what you are going to say with this colleague. If speaking from the heart isn't easy, write a script.

- Seek out your local Gay-Straight Alliance (some boards have these for staff). Seek out local support networks and attend an event or call for support. In the very early days of my coming out, I called a support network that connected me to events.

- Don't rush! Tell people in your own time and at your own pace.

- Ensure you have a group of friends outside of work that you can lean on. The reality is that not everyone you tell will take the news well. This is a reflection on them, not you.

- Cross your fingers and have hope in your heart that you won't need them, but learn who your union or association representative is and how to get hold of them if needed.

REFERENCES

Brown, B. (2018) *Dare to Lead*. New York: Random House.

Palmer, P. J. (1998) *Courage to Teach*. San Francisco, CA: Jossey-Bass.

PART 5
OWNING OUR BRAVERY

PART

5

22
BRAVE VULNERABILITY
Debra Rutley

KEY POINTS

This chapter will:

- Normalise experiences of mental illness;
- *Challenge* the established thinking on school leadership;
- Help you create a culture of understanding around mental health in your school.

INTRODUCTION

There is shame attached to talking about mental health. Being mentally unwell does not mean that you are not good enough. Being mentally unwell does not reflect on your ability to do your job. We need to *challenge* the narrative around mental health, and in writing this chapter I am rising to that *challenge*.

BEING SUPERWOMAN

When you take on the role of Superwoman, it's easy to run headfirst into burnout and then depression.

I was a deputy head and mother of two young boys when I experienced my first crash. Looking back, I had been balancing 'work' with 'life' by just doing the life bit as fast as I could. I was the archetypal 'human giver' (Nagoski and Nagoski, 2019), always solving other people's problems for them, and I loved the fact that people came to me for help. I invested a lot of my energy in other people and I thought self-care was lazy and selfish. Just being 'good enough' was never enough in any aspect of my life, and I had inadvertently created a culture at my school where it was easier for colleagues to come to me with their problems than to think of solutions for themselves.

The first time it hit me there were no warning signs. It was a normal school day. A colleague presented me with a problem that wasn't even particularly challenging, but it was the straw that broke the camel's back. I was in someone else's office and I started to cry. I didn't know why I was crying, I just knew I couldn't stop and I needed to go home.

Thinking about what happened next still fills me with 'fear'. I live in fear that I will be that ill again. My black hole was so deep it took me 18 months to get out of it. I cried. I slept and I spent months with my duvet, unable to talk to anyone. I was an empty shell of my former self, unrecognisable to family and friends. I was a bystander to life, able to observe but not allowed to join in. I felt nothing. I was away from work for a very long time, but I was so broken that I didn't even think about it and only focused on the most basic non-negotiables like getting my children to school and making sure they were fed. The rest of my time was spent in my bed.

I was very lucky to be surrounded by colleagues who supported my recovery and eventual return to work with love: they met me for coffee, and understood that it would take me three days to recover from the emotional effort of that meeting; they sent me notes and messages of compassion to remind me I wasn't forgotten. I was allowed to return at my own pace and I was allowed to have setbacks. These colleagues protected me and came together around me as a supportive *community* that accepted and embraced my vulnerability. Eventually, I felt stronger and wiser for having been through the trauma of severe depression and came out the other side a different person.

On my return to work, I couldn't hide. People knew why I had been off, and inside the safe haven of my school, I was open and honest about what had happened to me. I modelled the behaviours that had helped me recover with my staff, and made it easy to talk about mental health. I was better, I was strong, I had conquered depression and I had won. In retrospect, I felt superior about it: 'Look at me and how well I am … considering.' However, to those outside my school *community* I still explained my absence as 'exhaustion', never daring to use the word depression.

Over the following years, I would occasionally dip into and out of depression, but nobody else ever seemed to notice. Six years later, I took on the role of headteacher, and with that I felt a growing sense of needing to be strong for other people. Looking back, I can see how I tried to create a culture of openness around mental health for my staff, whilst at the same time concealing my own vulnerability. I was trying so hard to project the image of the person that I had once been, that nobody looked closely enough to realise that she was no longer there.

NOT LISTENING TO YOUR OWN ADVICE

The second time I crashed there were warning signs: I had become forgetful; I was struggling to read; and I had once again become intimate friends with my duvet. I tried to ignore them all but eventually found myself crying inconsolably with that now familiar and overwhelming feeling of not being able to cope. I was not in control.

From my previous experience, I knew that the first step of recovery is to acknowledge that you are not well and the second step is to tell someone. I told my Chair of Trustees, who was incredibly supportive, and insisted that I take off as long as I needed.

But, despite all that I'd read and said and done in the years since my first crash, I felt embarrassed as a leader; I felt ashamed.

I was worried my staff would also feel insecure in my absence. So, with the help of my Chair, I composed an email explaining what was happening with honesty, compassion and vulnerability. Although in my heart I knew this was the right thing to do, I still felt shame about sharing my story.

LOVE

The beautiful thing about working in my school is that shame has no power over students or staff. Instead, we explicitly talk about the transformational power of love, using it as a way to support others and encourage them to flourish. Love is our core value and is in abundance in all of our schools, and it is not dished out sparingly. In response to my email, my staff showered me with love. The whole school *community* showed me their care and support, in their own individual ways. They said the things to me that I had spent years saying to other members of staff, and it was the small gestures that meant the most: a text saying 'look after yourself'; an invitation for coffee; and some staff even being brave enough to give me advice. These small things made a huge difference and, collectively, they helped to pull me out of the black hole I was in.

However, I was afraid I'd never be able to face work again.

I was initially reluctant to accept medication for my depression, seeing that need as a further weakness. But slowly my perception *changed*. I came to understand that at times we all need some extra support, and, like fertiliser revitalising a delicate plant, medication can help us return to a healthy state. With medication, my brain started to work again. I gave myself permission to 'try' and slowly reassembled myself with lots of rest and self-care.

SELF-LOVE

When I came back at the start of the new academic year, there was a real sense of relief from the whole school *community*. This time I was more honest about myself and my illness. I shared my learning and I made wellbeing my priority. I spoke about myself in terms of vulnerability, rather than conquering adversity. Often, leaders who promote good mental health do so from the standpoint of being a saviour: 'I can look after you because I'm well. I'm strong.' I now lead from the opposite perspective: 'I can look after you because I understand. I am vulnerable.'

LEADING WITH LOVE

The biggest impact across the whole organisation was the realisation that my role had grown too big; it was the role that needed to *change*, not me.

Who I am today is enhanced by the self-awareness and the insight that come from the introspection of depression. It has made me a better headteacher, but I live in fear of it happening again, so I have consciously created a culture that values, talks about and promotes good mental health to protect both my colleagues and myself. This is a daily *challenge* and it takes courage and a constant expectation to be 10% braver.

At my school, we have created a culture and ethos where everyone looks out for each other, and it's OK not to be OK, whilst also providing staff with the tools and resources to support their own mental health.

Passing on being 10% braver

- Normalise: as a leader, you need to normalise mental ill health and you need to validate it as a 'real' illness. You need to empathise and notice your colleagues and seek to know more when something isn't right. You need a level of understanding that is deeper than awareness.

- Prevent: when you plan the whole school calendar, have staff wellbeing at the forefront of your mind. Support your staff to make their own wellbeing plans based on the peaks and troughs of the year and encourage them to reflect on their own needs and the needs of others. If you ask someone how they ended the term and they answer 'badly', help them to plan better for the next end of term. Ask them, how they want to feel at the end of this term.

- Recover: understand what your stressors are and what you need to do to recover from them. Be intentional about building in time to recover from a stressful day, week or term.

REFERENCE
Nagoski, E. and Nagoski, A. (2019) *Burnout: The Secret to Solving the Stress Cycle*. London: Vermillion.

23
BEING COMFORTABLE AND AUTHENTIC AS AN LGBT+ LEADER AND ROLE MODEL

Claire Neaves

KEY POINTS

Over the past few years, I've been on a journey which has led me to become more and more open about my place in the LGBT+ *community* and about my identity. This chapter will explain why I needed to be 10% braver:

- For myself: to fully accept who I was and to be able to lead authentically;
- For my peers: to build a *community* and collaborate with those like me;
- For my family: to show that I value, love and support them;
- For my students: to be a role model and to provide what I missed as a young person.

A NOTE ON THE SCOPE OF THIS CHAPTER

The first time I wrote publicly about LGBT+ issues, identifying myself as a member of the *community*, I stated that those 'under the LGBT+ umbrella will face both common and unique issues' (Nicholls, 2018). Whilst transgender teachers will face some of the issues raised in this chapter and some of the advice may be useful, sexuality and gender identity are distinct things and, whilst I stand fully in solidarity with the transgender *community*, I do not claim to speak for them and write only about my own experience.

INTRODUCTION

It's a badly kept secret that the ninth #WomenEd 'C' is cake. For those of us in the LGBT+ *community*, there's also a tenth: coming out. If you believe the popular narrative (which you really shouldn't), then this is a one-time thing. There's a huge build-up, a dramatic speech and then either joyful acceptance or hurtful rejection. It can absolutely be like that, especially for younger people coming out to a significant person in their life for the first time, but that's far from the end. It's a process that happens regularly. It can be public or private, tedious and mundane or important and liberating. It can be exhilarating but it can also be dangerous. It's sometimes planned, but often a split-second decision made in the course of a conversation. It's not universal, either. It's not a case of 'being out' or not. We are all part of multiple communities: family, neighbourhood, education or work, friendship groups, social clubs, and so on, and it is often the case that people in the LGBT+ *community* will be out to varying degrees in different spaces. As Sedgwick states, 'there are remarkably few of even the most openly gay people who are not deliberately in the closet with someone personally or economically or institutionally important to them' (2008: 67–8).

TO COME OUT OR NOT?

If we're not all out to everyone, how do we make this decision? Many people outside of the *community* question why people feel the need to share their sexuality at all. Shouldn't that kind of thing be kept private? Especially in a work environment and when you work with children? This is where the double standards start to apply. Sexuality isn't all about sex. We may define ourselves by our attraction, but in practical terms this often means who we are in a relationship with or who our potential partners may be. Heterosexual people don't ever describe talking about their relationships as 'coming out' but they signal their relationship status and sexuality to others in a variety of ways: a wedding band, a mention of 'my husband' or a family photo in an office. Heterosexual people often don't think twice about discussing their partners in the staffroom and may mention them in anecdotes in the classroom, yet they are never accused of playing identity politics or flaunting their sexuality.

It's naïve to suggest that those of us who are lesbian, gay, bisexual or other marginalised sexualities are making a choice to not keep our private lives private. We just want to participate in the same conversations as our colleagues. Often a simple question or assumption about a spouse, or how childcare works in our families, prompts a choice; correct the person speaking and thus come out, or let it slide and effectively lie to our colleagues. We also exist in spaces outside of the workplace. What do we say to students who have seen us with a partner in a public place? If 'the family is understood to be synonymous with heterosexual and monogamous relationships' (Holt, 2019), then how do those of us outside of these norms participate in these conversations without changing the narrative? If we don't *challenge* assumptions, then we also give weight to the argument that our lives are not suitable to be shared and that our relationships and identities don't have equal value.

A BALANCING ACT

Despite the huge strides made in recent years, the evidence shows that we are far from having created an equitable society. Badgett et al. found 'resounding evidence of harmful experiences for LGBT people across multiple aspects of their daily lives' (2019: 11). More specifically, the government states that 'research and evidence has continued to suggest that LGBT people face discrimination, bullying and harassment in education, at work and on the streets, hate crime and higher inequalities in health satisfaction and outcomes' (Government Equalities Office, 2019).

This is particularly true for certain parts of the *community*: 'bisexual and trans people are consistently shown to have the worst health' (Barker and Iantaffi, 2019: 23). Every person in the LGBT+ *community* will have a personal tale of abuse, harassment or discrimination. Most of us have several. When coming out, there is always a question of safety. How will this person react? Will it make things worse? Is my job at risk? By being more visible, we open ourselves to more of the negative responses.

This may be why passing as heterosexual is sometimes referred to as a privilege. However, harm is present in other ways. There is a constant tension between seeking safety and being inauthentic, which can have a significant impact on our mental health. For the first ten years of my career, I was part of the 56% who were not open about their sexuality in the workplace (Government Equalities Office, 2019). Eventually, I could no longer pretend. I feared that by not correcting colleagues' assumptions I was indirectly adding to the stigma faced by the *community*. I was also consumed with guilt at hiding something that was no longer a source of shame. I felt I was letting my chosen family down by not being open about them.

In 2015, I attended the first #WomenEd unconference and, in a session on authentic leadership, realised that I wasn't supporting myself or others by not being open. That year I began a process of coming out which has included tweeting, blogging, writing, addressing students and being honest with staff at a new school. The process isn't finished, and it hasn't been easy. Telling some family members has been tough and some are still unaware. There are relationships I've lost in the process, but I've found myself.

BEING A ROLE MODEL

It is easy in 2020 to be dismissive about coming out and to label authenticity as a fad. However, it is of real value not only for ourselves but also for those around us. Being out and visible increases the chances of younger LGBT+ people, those questioning their sexuality or those unable to come out, knowing that we are a source of guidance and support. We can make *connection*s with those who need us and engage in mutually supportive relationships. Building communities is an antidote to the alienation we can often feel.

However, we must acknowledge that it's not simple. Whilst being a gay or lesbian teacher may not be the talk of the staffroom it once was, we must not view coming out as easy or as an obligation. It is still an intensely personal act, and it matters. Medford points out that '"Who cares!?!" is not consciously harmful rhetoric ... but ... to dismiss the coming out process for a gay person, particularly a young black man in the public eye, is an ignorant, privileged stance to take' (2019). This statement, referring to the rapper Lil Nas X, reminds us of 'the many intersecting privileges and oppressions which make it far easier and safer for some people to be out than others' (Barker and Iantaffi, 2019: 76). As Small states, many are not out about their sexuality because they belong to 'visible minority groups and don't want to add something else that they feel will count against them' (2019).

A LASTING LEGACY

Whilst being 10% braver, coming out and leading authentically can be a source of support to individuals, peers and pupils, there are still so many of our *community* who feel unable to take this step. An intersectional lens, as described above, explains why many with overlapping protected characteristics or other marginalised identities may not feel safe to, but for those of us with relative privilege in many other ways, why does it still feel so radical? For those my age, our experience of education is important. In the United Kingdom, until 2003 (2001 in Scotland) a clause in 'the Local Government Act 1988 banned the "promotion" of homosexuality by local authorities and in Britain's schools' (Sommerlad, 2018). This represents the whole of my schooling, from early years to further education, and I am only now realising how much this shaped my life and my choices as a young woman. It was impossible for me to imagine a future as anything close to what I felt inside, so I suppressed my feelings and taught myself to ignore lingering doubts.

Sommerlad argues that the 'pernicious influence of the clause unquestionably played a huge role in legitimising hate and reinforcing playground homophobia and bullying, demonising LGBT+ children and ensuring many stayed imprisoned in the closet for fear of social reprisals or disapproval' (2018). In addition to this, I certainly experienced, as Stewart details, 'limited access to information about same-sex relationships' and 'the feeling of shame and isolation' (2019). With repeal though did not come *change*, and many of the teachers who taught under the act, and those of us who were educated under it, are still feeling the ramifications. Small notes that Section 28 'added to my internalised homophobia. People my age, and especially those who are now teachers, are still living with the fallout from this' (2019). There is ongoing confusion and fear around how and what to teach in terms of LGBT+ issues, which has allowed homophobes to capitalise on doubt and sow division.

Waugh writes that '[w]hat remains with me now is the unspoken distancing I experienced' (2014), and it is protecting LGBT+ students from this sadness that motivates me to be authentic and open at work, to deliver the education and provide the safe space that I desperately needed. I agree with Small that the 'real onus should be on schools to create an environment that makes staff and students feel safe enough to be honest about their sexuality' (2019). When looking at the implications of the harm caused to LGBT+ people, the effects have also been measured beyond the personal. Badgett et al.'s research found that '[n]ot only are these violations and forms of exclusionary treatment harmful to the individuals involved, they also carry costs that impact the broader economy' (2019:12). It seems logical, then, that institutions should be invested in reducing harm. Our schools are a good place to start.

We cannot leave it to isolated educators, or worse, LGBT+ students, to create the conditions for equality. I'd urge you all to be 10% braver and shape your school communities. *Change* will come, not through people like me telling their stories (though that may help), but through a shift in culture, where we are all supported and celebrated.

Passing on being 10% braver

- Remember that you don't have to come out to effect *change*: you can be a valuable ally to both students and peers by raising LGBT+ issues in schools and helping others make *connections*.

- Be prepared for pushback: schools are often very traditional and conservative environments. Know what you want to communicate and *challenge* where you can.

- Know where your boundaries are: have clarity about what is acceptable to you and be confident in saying no when you need to.

- You need role models too: find a *community* and collaborate with people who will support you.

REFERENCES

Badgett, M. V. L., Waaldijk, K. and Rodgers, Y. V. D. M. (2019) 'The relationship between LGBT inclusion and economic development: Macro-level evidence', *World Development*, *120*: 1–14.

Barker, M.-J. and Iantaffi, A. (2019) *Life Isn't Binary: On Being Both, Beyond and In-between*. London: Jessica Kingsley.

Government Equalities Office (2019) *National LGBT Survey: Summary Report*. London: Government Equalities Office.

Holt, M. (2019) '"God save the queer": Discussing the role of the family in international relations', *E-International Relations*, 7 July [Online]. Available at: www.e-ir.info/2019/07/07/god-save-the-queer-discussing-the-role-of-the-family-in-international-relations (accessed 29 October 2019).

Medford, G. (2019) 'Kevin Hart's treatment of Lil Nas X proves straight people still aren't listening', *Gal-Dem*, 6 September [Online]. Available at: http://gal-dem.com/kevin-hart-lil-nas-x-lgbtqi/?sfns=mo (accessed 28 October 2019).

Nicholls, C. (2018) 'Making the choice to role model', *LGBT Ed*, 5 June [Online]. Available at: http://lgbted.uk/?p=507 (accessed 28 October 2019).

Sedgwick, E. K. (2008) *Epistemology of the Closet*, 2nd edition. London: University of California Press.

Small, I. (2019) 'I don't blame any teacher for not coming out as gay', *The Guardian*, 20 August [Online]. Available at: www.theguardian.com/education/2019/aug/20/i-dont-blame-any-teacher-for-not-coming-out-as-gay?CMP=twt_a-education_b-gdnedu (accessed 28 October 2019).

Sommerlad, J. (2018) 'Section 28: What was Margaret Thatcher's controversial law and how did it affect the lives of LGBT+ people?', *The Independent*, 24 May [Online]. Available at: www.independent.co.uk/news/uk/politics/section-28-explained-lgbt-education-schools-homosexuality-gay-queer-margaret-thatcher-a8366741.html (accessed 30 October 2019).

Stewart, H. (2019) 'Why do we need LGBTQ teachers to be visible in our schools?', *Means Happy*, 10 August [Online]. Available at: https://meanshappy.com/why-do-we-need-lgbtq-teachers-to-be-visible-in-our-schools (accessed 28 October 2019).

Waugh, C. (2014) 'Who I am, what I do', *Christopher Waugh*, 31 May [Online]. Available at: https://chris.edutronic.net/who-i-am-what-i-do (accessed 28 October 2019).

24
ASYLUM
Felicity King

KEY POINTS

This chapter will:

- Show how a frightening personal situation became the catalyst to taking charge of my wellbeing in all aspects of my life;
- Introduce the personal development approach I felt was missing in the way we develop our teachers;
- Illustrate how I stepped away from traditional problem-solving consultancy to truly nurture teams and individuals from the inside out.

INTRODUCTION

I had been on my knees for weeks, only this time I was on the cold kitchen floor. I can't remember what day it was. They all seemed the same. I was exhausted from lack of sleep and found myself riding shotgun with the clock, in the security that bedtime would be there eventually. Somehow bedtime brought an end to the fire of panic inside me. Whilst it didn't burn out completely, it did at least seem at arm's length for a few hours. It meant my shame was tucked away under the duvet. No one else could see it. No one else needed to know, least of all my children.

This night was different though. The grenade of shame so buried inside me meant I *was* going to explode. I couldn't take this anymore. I searched for *asylum* and entered our postcode so I could find a place nearby. Driving the car had become a problem. No, to be honest, getting in the car had become a problem and that was just for me. Getting the boys in the car was itself a job for an army. So, it had to be somewhere close. The magic rainbow doughnut whirled round on the screen and then it popped up, only asylum turned out to be a nightclub in Hull.

THE MOTHER OF ALL IMPOSTERS

Not what I was expecting but, like a bolt of lightning to the head, that night *changed* everything. Here was the gap between the conveyor belts of paralysing thought, the mother of all imposters and the noise in my previously capable, career-woman head.

That simple moment invited a new chain of thought and one that prompted feelings that weren't feelings of anxiety anymore.

You might be wondering why I'm sharing this story of post-natal distress? Well, the cold, hard touch of the kitchen floor is a place where I was on my knees. And then I got up. Then the work started. And from that place of discomfort came hope and the realisation that so much of what I went through could be equally powerful in the way we look after our teachers. So being 10% braver for me is about shouting from the rooftops that our teachers must come first. From that moment, I completely *changed* the way I lived and worked. Adversity inspired *change* and commitment, just like the #WomenEd values we share today. Instead of being the education consultant with tools and tips to solve a problem, I turned back to the simple way our thoughts can be so powerful in creating our feelings. I had to hit my reset button on the floor that night and I've done it a million times since. I had to allow my thinking to *change* so I had the energy to get up and look after my babies. And, in the same, brave way, my work shifted to pointing teachers back to their foundations to give them access to that same clarity, self-kindness and calm.

I hope I can share how re-claiming your brain is the vital link to sustaining yourself and your colleagues. This is about cutting yourself some slack and living bravely from the inside out.

THE WELLBEING BAR

Living my 10% braver was about to become real and those #WomenEd values around *confidence, collaboration* and coming together were about to be tested. Knowing something is wrong and doing something about it are separated by a dark and prickly void, a bit like walking through a cactus greenhouse with the lights turned off. I knew my school improvement work was all about outputs. I also knew that the popular approach of measure, improve and measure again did nothing to nurture and bolster the people at the heart of my work. If the so-called support didn't serve to raise the wellbeing and engagement of the teachers, how on earth could it lead to sustained adaptation and truly human leadership going forward? How could we deliver our vision for our students if we didn't have a vision for the way we looked after our staff?

In simple terms, I had experienced, first hand, just how powerful my thoughts were in creating emotions. Professor of Psychology Jeffrey Nevid explains how emotions follow on from thoughts and, without thoughts as drivers, emotions are much lighter to tolerate (Nevid, 2014). I can relate to this first hand and, over time, the feelings became more uncomfortable and the default setting was to try to push away or suppress them, as quickly as possible. The problem was that the more I pushed the feelings away, the louder the voice of inadequacy grew in my head. And so the cycle continued until my wheels came off.

There are many ways that thoughts show up and create resistance for us. I don't know about you but, given the right encouragement, a lack of sleep, niggling cold or a pile of marking, I can think myself into all sorts of doom and indeed out of the healthy, energy-giving options that would do me the power of good. Picture a dark, rainy evening, the fire is lit and yet I'm supposed to be going to spin class. If my thinking is that way out, it's the sofa and fireside for me! We are the masters of thought constipation. So, why don't we take them for what they are and simply become great at observing them? Here's a plan to get you started right now.

For the fastest results, you might like to practise this as you read it and then as many times as you can over the next few days. That way, when the more negative and debilitating thoughts set in, you're a dab hand with the technique and have it in your arsenal:

- When you notice the critical self-talk, slow down your breathing and focus on the in and out breath. Rather than listening to the words, try to focus on the feeling created in your body.
- Notice the location and how it feels. Use simple, observational language to really take away the judgement factor. I call this gagging Simon Cowell!
- Focus on the sensation. Let's say, for me, it's a hot, prickly and tight sensation in my throat and neck.
- Now, open up to welcoming that sensation into your body as if it were a guest. A guest visits and then leaves again; it will not stay forever.
- Finally, take those sensations on a tour of your body, quite literally a guided tour. I start at the top of my head and work my way down. I channel an estate agent's talk and go around each body part, as if it were the rooms in my house. I can honestly say, in the best part of a decade, I have never managed to get to my toes.
- Within a few minutes, the sensations wear off and the quiet, clear and confident mind emerges. I'm no longer feeling my thinking. You could say I've lined up my #WomenEd ducks!

Some of you might be thinking that this sounds like mindfulness and it's not something you and your staff favour. I have nothing against mindfulness at all but, honestly, this is much simpler. This is getting comfortable with the uncomfortable feelings that will invariably crop up in life. If they didn't, we wouldn't be alive. The real problem is that sometimes they are so uncomfortable, painful even, that our default is to try to suppress them or bat them away. Getting comfortable with the bodily sensations – good, bad or ugly – completes the feedback loop to our brain and enables it to operate from a place of neuroplasticity and capacity. I can highly recommend the work of Dr Rick Hanson, who demonstrates how to grow lasting happiness, resilience and purpose (Hanson, 2018). Here's what I say to my 5-year-old son: 'Your brain needs fuel to work properly and part of that fuel is seeing the full range of sensations whizzing around in your body. It's like pressing reset inside your head. This is just how it works.'

Taking the technique outlined above into your life, the nature of thought becomes known and felt. As my own coach suggested many years ago, once you know something, you can't un-know it. I suppose it's a bit like the tooth fairy not being real.

MISSING LINKS AND RETAINING TEACHERS

Looking back at the tricky times in my career and personal life, having this foundation on board and up front would have made a world of difference. The retention statistics tell a sad story, as 'almost a third of school leaders are now leaving within three years of taking up the post' (Turner, 2018), there are 'fewer full-time equivalent secondary teachers than at any point since 2010' (Ward, 2019a) and nearly 'one in three teachers leave the classroom within five years of starting teaching' (Ward, 2019b).

It's so easy to become locked in a mindset of inevitable workload, personal sacrifice and being permanently on the go. And we still focus on output and measuring at the expense of nurturing what is innate in us all. Re-framing my consultancy practice was a no-brainer. I simply plug teachers back into their innate resilience, taking away that energy-draining conflict. It works because it's how we work, so it's fast and it delivers.

To be a mum, I had to find a way to know when to listen to the thoughts in my head and when to hit the reset button. To lead in a classroom or indeed a school today, we must find a way to take care of ourselves from the inside out and empower our colleagues to do the same. If there is one little chunk of science we might like to shine a light on every day, then how about we make it this? We don't have to be afraid of our own experience – most of it is created through thought and if we wait, for the briefest of moments, a new one of those is sure to come along.

THE WISDOM OF #WOMENED

A wise woman once told me this: you don't have to know everything to know what's right, and that must start with knowing what's right for you. When that's in place and you check in with it often, you'll be all right. Let's not forget that being all right isn't always easy, it requires being brave and it deserves commitment. Sometimes you only need to be 10% braver and, at other times, it seems like you're throwing everything up in the air and being 110% braver. It's those days you remember – not for being rewarded, promoted or thanked but for knowing you adapted when you needed to, and asked for help from those people with an eye for your vision and a heart for your needs. It's those days that you gather strength and momentum. It's those days that you move forward one step at a time, with clarity, self-kindness and trust. And always, always, from the inside out.

Passing on being 10% braver

- Be an internal observer rather than an evaluator and notice what shifts for you. #change
- Through sharing your story and being 10% braver, you can nurture your family, friends and colleagues to do the same. #connection
- Create a little bit of time every day to share this foundation through your classrooms and *community*. #clarity

REFERENCES

Hanson, R. (2018) *Resilient: 12 Tools for Transforming Everyday Experiences into Lasting Happiness*. New York: Harmony Books.

Nevid, J. (2014) *Essentials of Psychology: Concepts and Applications*. Boston, MA: Wadsworth Publishing.

Turner, C. (2018) 'Almost a third of headteachers now leave within three years, official data shows', *The Telegraph*, 5 May [Online]. Available at: www.telegraph.co.uk/education/2018/05/05/almost-third-headteachers-now-leave-within-three-years-official (accessed 3 April 2020).

Ward, H. (2019a) 'Number of secondary teachers in England drops again', *tes*, 27 June [Online]. Available at: tes.com/news/number-secondary-teachers-england-drops-again (accessed 3 April 2020).

Ward, H. (2019b) 'One in three teachers leaves within five years', *tes*, 27 June [Online]. Available at: www.tes.com/news/one-three-teachers-leaves-within-five-years (accessed 3 April 2020).

25

SLAYING THE DRAGON OF IMPOSTER SYNDROME

Imogen Senior

KEY POINTS

This chapter will:

- Reveal how imposter syndrome undermines women in education;
- Show how fear of being found out limits growth;
- Explore facing imposter syndrome in challenging situations;
- Celebrate the value of being brave and facing your fears.

INTRODUCTION

After a swift journey into senior leadership, I felt that I needed to demonstrate at every turn my right to my role. Feeling out of my depth, I lived in fear of being found out and making a huge mistake. Gradually, I became established and stayed in the same role for seven years. At that point, facing dramatic *changes* in my school, I had to decide whether to hide in my areas of expertise or to take a leap of faith, to be braver. I decided that it was better to choose my own future, even if that meant fighting the nagging internal voice that told me I had already overstretched my ability. I needed to face and attempt to slay the dragon of imposter syndrome.

AN IMPOSTER IN PLAIN SIGHT?

Several years ago, in my first significant leadership role, the head came into my office. We were chatting and he looked (slightly puzzled) around the office at the wall of thank you cards I kept on every noticeboard and surface. I explained I kept the cards, letters and scribbled notes from students, parents and colleagues so that I had proof that I was good at my job. 'What!?', he said, 'Surely you know you're good at this job?' The truth was, despite my professional performance and experience, I still expected to be outed as an imposter. Somehow the cards gave me the headspace to do my job in the knowledge that I had got away with it so far. The head thought I was knowledgeable, professional and diligent but I felt that I was just an imposter, pretending to be those things.

When Clance and Imes wrote about imposter syndrome in high-achieving women in the 1970s, they identified the 'secret sense' that the women did not really belong (1978: 241). Although the context of women in the workplace has *changed* in the 40 years since, my personal experience is that competent women in education still doubt their abilities to a far greater extent than male colleagues do. Mohr's oft-quoted article for the *Harvard Business Review* showed that women tend to apply for jobs only when they believe that they meet all the criteria (Mohr, 2014). In my career, this need to prove my credentials from the start has been absolute. In meetings, I would often keep quiet unless I was sure I could substantiate my own view with verifiable evidence. My instinct was to avoid taking a risk in an application for fear of being caught out at interview or, worse still, getting a job I could not do.

I have now gone further in my career than I ever dreamed, but to do so I had to take more risks than I was comfortable with. Imposter syndrome made me doubt that I deserved a leadership role and made me miss out on opportunities to grow and develop my career. I did not apply for posts that would require me to lead existing colleagues as I believed that others were more qualified than I to be leaders. I pursued CPD in areas I already knew rather than trying to broaden my knowledge, as I wanted to prove I knew what I was doing. In time, the fear of being an imposter in my first leadership role subsided. My experience and success gave me security and, although this didn't extend to taking steps into new areas, I felt some degree of *confidence*. I believed that I could do my existing job but was hesitant about applying for a next step. I stayed away from the dragon, safe behind a shield of experience, and made no real attempt to even fight, let alone slay, it. Then, my role was abruptly considered for redundancy and I found myself asking challenging questions that would decide my future. Did I really deserve to be in a leadership role? How could I evidence my ability? Did I have the skills I needed?

I knew that I had to face those old fears to move forwards. So, in a rare demonstration of bravery, I resigned from my post and faced my uncertain future, determined to be braver than I had ever been.

TIME TO RE-EVALUATE

Faced with a 'crunch' moment, I had to decide if there was real evidence that I was an imposter and attempt to find the *confidence* to take the right next steps. To gain peace of mind, I wanted to assess whether there was evidence that I had achieved any level of success in my own right. I have always told students that the first step in dealing with anxiety is to call out our fears to see if they really are concerns. I decided that I needed to do a career appraisal to see where my worries really lay. I started with my academic qualifications, what I had achieved and whether I could have got them by something other than my own effort or ability. I have four qualifications from three different universities and had to admit to myself that it was unlikely all of these were flukes. That initial step was genuinely liberating. I had berated myself for years that I should have worked harder, and I had compared myself to a standard that was not based on any actual examples I had encountered. I had hidden behind my qualifications, like I hid behind thank you cards, and didn't accept that I deserved them through my own merit or that they were a demonstration of any aptitude.

I went on from there. I looked at each role I had fulfilled, what I was proud of and where I felt I had not done a great job. I realised that I was discounting my own impact and expected more from myself than was realistic. I had felt I needed to make up for time when I had been on maternity leave to justify coming back into a senior role, and that in doing so I had taken a back seat at times. This sense of diminished status for mothers is well documented. Correll et al.'s research suggests that mothers 'are judged by a harsher standard than nonmothers' in the workplace (2007: 1302). Whilst I was not conscious of this from others, I had certainly held myself to a higher standard which contributed to my lack of belonging. Feeling like an imposter is not an exclusively female experience but, for me, it is linked to my experience as a woman and mother. I didn't give myself an easy ride at any point of my analysis and tried to be objective. I wanted to really think about whether I had been faking it or deserved credit for the things that had gone well in my career. In short, I mentally picked myself up and dusted myself down. I saw that, whilst I wasn't perfect, my success had not been an accident. I was not a total imposter; in fact, I was a leader.

NECESSITY AS THE MOTHER OF INVENTION

It is easier to be brave when you don't have a choice. Resigning from my role removed the luxury of self-doubt and meant that financially I had to act. Whether I felt brave or not, I had to apply for jobs. My husband and I have three young children, my husband's job was also under threat and we are very much tied to a specific geographic area. With the clock ticking, I read job descriptions and filled in application forms like there was no tomorrow. What I found, to my frustration, was that I could not predict the response. I applied for jobs that were well within my established skill set as well as those that were completely new. I wrote apologetic letters, almost defeatistly throwing my hat into the ring for jobs at all levels. This was not a great strategy. What I found was that I got interviews for the senior jobs but I got no response for the jobs I knew I could do easily. This was how I found myself applying for headships, not because I felt ready, but because finally I could see that I met the specification and I recognised that I had something to offer. Going into my first headship interview, my primary fear was that I would look foolish and massively out of my depth. In truth, I hoped that I would make a decent impression so that I might stand a chance at any other roles that came up and get some good interview experience. As the process went on, I was utterly terrified that I might be offered the job and be unable to do it, but, after several interviews, I realised that I really could be a head and that was what I wanted to be. I was so concerned with not looking foolish that I did not visit schools before I applied, which I now know was a huge mistake. I was very fortunate that I was given good advice at that point. I realise now how important *connection* is. I spoke with experienced female leaders who gave me guidance on what to emphasise in applications and on the need to abandon my apologist stance. Over time, I realised that I needed to be devastated if I didn't get the job, because I had to accept that I stood a chance. I was no longer an imposter making up the numbers; I was a real candidate, I was fighting the dragon.

TRUSTING MY GUT INSTINCT, NOT INNER DOUBT

Teaching can be a lonely job because so much of what we do is in our own classrooms and, although I have always worked with brilliant people, I was amazed at how much help, support and guidance I was given from all quarters and especially the *community* of women who were behind me offering support. I was given pragmatic advice from those who had been in similar situations as well as all manner of practical help. From the experience of other women through #WomenEd, I knew that I could have a place in school leadership and that I could stop internally apologising for my perceived failings.

Ultimately, in order to get over the nagging doubt that I didn't belong, I had to trust in my own abilities. I am far from the finished article, but I am no longer an imposter in the role. Being brave, in my case, wasn't a bungee jump of fear and instant reward but a series of steps forward with a different approach. The experience showed me that I can trust my gut instinct and abilities. Rather than finding myself jobless as I feared, I got a one-term contract in an independent school, teaching my own subject at GCSE and A level. I relished the new *challenge*: specifications I had not taught before, a completely new school system and environment, new colleagues and new students. The experience reminded me of what a great and refreshing opportunity *change* can be and how important it is to be in the right school. I made a conscious decision that I would pursue my career in a Catholic school, if possible, and when a post soon appeared, I was successfully appointed.

Dear reader, two terms later I was appointed as headteacher at the same school.

SLAYING MY DRAGON

In fighting my dragon, I've learned that, as a headteacher, I need to know where I have genuine weaknesses, but I can't be paralysed by them and must accept that I am in my post for a reason. I occasionally check the sign at the front of the school to really believe that I am a headteacher. I sometimes still feel that someone is going to appear and turf me out the door, but mostly I am revelling in keeping up with my role and its *challenge*s.

I am honest about my limitations and abilities as I was throughout the selection process. I respect those who appointed me as well as those who also applied for the job. If all else fails, I can take refuge in research. Sakulku and Alexander argue that 'most impostors are able to fulfil their academic or work requirements despite their self-perceived fraudulence' (2011: 76). Armed with this knowledge and the faith that guides me in my role, I now know that I am not an imposter.

My mum died just before I started as a headteacher. I am grateful that she knew I'd been appointed and relieved she knew how my story turned out, but it was a bittersweet time. Just before she died, I told her about something I was working on and she said, 'You know, you are going to be really good at this job'. That's the seal of approval that I carry the most. I am the woman who got the job, so I will get on with it.

Passing on being 10% braver

- Name your fear: analyse your strengths and weaknesses and whether these are reasonable assessments.
- If people you respect think you are doing a good job, recognise that you are.
- Be prepared for disappointment but don't accept it beforehand: always see yourself as a contender.
- Take support and advice but trust your own instincts and abilities. You did not get where you are by accident but because you are capable and talented.

REFERENCES

Clance, P. and Imes, S. (1978) 'The imposter phenomenon in high achieving women: Dynamics and therapeutic intervention', *Psychotherapy Theory Research and Practice*, 15: 241–7.

Correll, S. J., Benard, S. and Paik, I. (2007) 'Getting a job: Is there a motherhood penalty?' *The American Journal of Sociology*, 112(5): 1297–338.

Mohr, T. (2014) 'Why women don't apply for jobs unless they're 100% qualified', *Harvard Business Review*, 25 August [Online]. Available at: https://hbr.org/2014/08/why-women-dont-apply-for-jobs-unless-theyre-100-qualified%20(10%20December%202019)%20_ (accessed 10 December 2019).

Sakulku, J. and Alexander, J. (2011) 'The imposter phenomenon', *International Journal of Behavioral Science*, 6(1): 75–97.

26
MOVING MINDSETS AND FAILING FORWARD

Melissa Egri McCauley and Jacinta Calzada-Mayronne

KEY POINTS

This chapter will:

- Show we had to be 10% braver to join the hierarchy of educational leadership;
- Demonstrate how the value of failing forward and shifting our mindsets enabled us to grow;
- Reveal why we need women to be supportive of other women;
- Determine the impact that mentorship and sisterhood in supportive leadership can have on our successes.

INTRODUCTION

There is a disproportionate representation of women in the upper echelons of education, despite being a majority in the workplace. Data collected by the National Center for Education Statistics (NCES) shows that, in 2017, there were approximately 3.6 million full-time-equivalent elementary and secondary school teachers in the United States (NCES, 2017). Across the United States in 2015, 74% of K-12 public school teachers and 52% of public school principals were women; however, just over 24% of superintendents (the head of a public school district) were women (NCES, 2017). Why aren't more of the 74% of women climbing the ladder? Many studies in this area have repeatedly affirmed that the amount of support women receive has a significant impact on their leadership journey (Egri McCauley, 2019).

The adverse effects of feeling unsupported can damage the professional trajectory of women. Early on in Melissa's career, the idea of leadership was always her ambition, but, with a lack of support, she cast it aside due to a lack of *confidence* in her own abilities. Women can encounter oppressive experiences when climbing the ladder toward educational leadership. Some women pursuing leadership roles encounter adverse experiences from other women leaders within the field. In Jacinta's experience, in US public charter schools, male leaders were not as prevalent as female leaders. Women often appeared intimidated by the education and credentials that other women brought to the table. In this chapter, we celebrate the power of supporting one another and how women can positively lead other women as mentors and supporters as part of their leadership role. This chapter offers guidance on how, whilst failing forward, you can attain the support you need to climb the leadership ladder successfully, and why it is necessary to encourage each other to be 10% braver.

FAILING FORWARD AND MOVING MINDSETS

Women work vigorously to get to the top to achieve success in leadership positions, and research suggests that this causes some women to be reluctant to share or further the success of other women (Elias, 2018). The reason women are unwilling to share their success is due to feeling threatened by other women who are equally ambitious and who have a similar tenacity. Consequently, the reluctance to share success with other women can be harmful to the reputation of both women. Dr Jacqueline Pfluger Coccia, president of a nonpublic school, found that participants who also identified as women leaders felt 'the most discouraging and upsetting examples of bias in the workplace involved the mistreatment of women by other women' (2019: 112). This is known as the queen bee phenomenon, which is more specifically defined as 'the tendency of women leaders to assimilate into male-dominated organizations ... by distancing themselves from junior women and legitimizing inequality' (Derks et al., 2016: 456).

Jacinta often ran into the queen bee phenomenon. She began teaching a little later than most teachers, at the age of 26, and already had a Masters degree. She was an alternate route candidate and very tenacious – completing multiple programmes simultaneously. She completed an alternate route programme whilst also working towards her second Masters in Special Education and completed her second Masters whilst beginning work towards her doctoral degree. Along her journey, principals and direct supervisors all agreed that she was good at her job, but she often felt like a failure because the women to whom she directly reported belittled her. Jacinta was told that she had a bravado for being confident and was disrespectful in setting boundaries. These same women asked her if she was coming for their jobs and told her that she would never reach the positions she wanted and worked so hard to acquire. Instead of being supportive and utilising her expertise as an asset, she was berated.

Within the queen bee phenomenon, 'women are more likely to demonstrate more support for their peers [men within the field of education] than subordinates because they consider these women to have made similar sacrifices for career success' (Faniko et al., 2017: 647), leaving women who aspire to be in similar positions to fail or find other avenues to reach success, like pursuing advanced degrees. Being afraid to fail, that's exactly what Jacinta did to advance her career. In hindsight, Jacinta realised that her tenacity and ambition caused other women to be insecure, exhibiting the queen bee trait because they were also afraid to fail.

The reluctance to support another woman is not due to a personal vendetta; it's because women are afraid to fail. Women should focus on being 10% braver when reaching for those goals, whilst not being afraid of falling short. Regardless of the circumstances, women can achieve the success they desire, given they have the proper mindset to be tenacious for themselves. Being unafraid of failure can increase the *confidence* needed to step on to the climbing wall or ascend that ladder. Women need to understand that shortcomings are really failing forward, and failing forward is a lesson learned. The harder we fail, the less afraid we become of the what-ifs that can plague our minds. Failing is inevitable, yet the act of moving forward sets the tone for the resilience and the *confidence* to succeed. So, let's all fail forward. Don't tiptoe around your goals because of the possibility of failing. There are lessons to be learned around failing, which will lead to success. Not trying is also failure.

Clarity, confidence, community and *connection* helped Jacinta to be 10% braver. In her doctoral programme, where she met Melissa, she found a *community* of women who were on the same path to being 10% braver. They all knew what they wanted out of attaining their doctoral degrees, they were confident and took the risk of possibly failing but pushing forward anyway, and, importantly, they leaned on each other. The *community* and *connection* that they made are the reasons that you can call all four of them doctors. Strong women are the ones building each other up, not tearing each other down.

Melissa and Jacinta learned that shifting one's mindset and maturing a mental model that supports others can be beneficial for both parties, as well as opening the door for networking, seeking and providing advice. *Letting Go* (Scharmer, 2016) of an unsupportive mental model involves determining the mindset required, implementing the action and thinking accordingly. We can cultivate a more supportive mindset; being attentive, building good habits and adopting leadership mindset styles that promote the growth of others are the foundational steps. We didn't let the lack of support hold us back, and neither should you.

MENTORSHIP IN SUPPORTIVE LEADERSHIP

Research suggests that women who are aspiring leaders in the field of education may have more success and access to opportunities if they are mentored (Dunbar and Kinnersley, 2011). Unfortunately, this was not Melissa's experience at all; she lacked the mentorship she so desperately sought. From the beginning of her career, starting in the early childhood daycare system, she always wanted to be a leader. However, surrounded by men and unsure of herself, she was very cautious, lacked *confidence*, and therefore remained quiet most of the time. Not having that strong female presence to guide her, support her dreams or believe in her really affected her ambition. Although most of the staff in the education world were female teachers, there were few supportive women colleagues, and the leaders in the upper echelons of educational organisations were predominantly men. The value of a supportive network for women

to attain leadership positions, such as principal, assistant superintendent and/or superintendent, is crucial to women achieving these positions. In the United States, where 75% of teachers are women, men occupy over 75% of the leadership positions (Dana and Bourisaw, 2006). Eventually, finding the tenacity within and pushing forward on her own, Melissa enrolled in a doctoral programme, thanks to a former female teacher, turned colleague, turned friend, Ms M.

Whilst in the programme, Melissa found the support of more strong women, who had the same goals, ambitions and mindset. These women were wives, full-time employees and mothers, and had just as many things to juggle as she did. They understood her journey and provided Melissa with the *community* of support she so desperately needed; they encouraged and pushed her to speak up, and go after that leadership role. This group of women joined forces, celebrated their triumphs, lifted one another back up after their failures, remained focused and built a *connection* of strong, independent and educated women. This *community* of women were going to *change* the world by squashing the stigma of queen bee female leaders and tackling the inequality in the upper echelons of educational leadership.

Mentoring is defined as a 'developmental relationship that is embedded within the career context' (Ragins and Kram, 2007: 5). When it comes to women being supported and mentored, the impact can be immense. Mentoring is beneficial because it fosters the skills, experience and talent in developing women leaders within the field of education. While Melissa initially lacked a true mentoring partnership, the women she found along her doctoral journey offered her similar attributes. Not only did her *confidence* level soar, she pursued a leadership role in her district and was promoted to vice principal. She now has a better understanding of the value of the female support system and the impact it can have.

The question is, for women in education, what are the barriers to advancement, and what can women do to address these barriers? Melissa knows that she belongs at the leadership table, and if there isn't room for her, she will pull up a chair. She also makes it a personal mission to support other women and continues to foster those positive relationships, whilst encouraging them to find *confidence* within themselves. Traditionally, one barrier that has restricted women from advancing in their careers is professional socialisation. Professional socialisation is an additional layer of mentorship and support where aspiring leaders are exposed to and can internalise the social construct of the upper echelons of education. Preparing future women leaders by providing mentorship and the opportunity to engage in leadership will break down the barrier of advancement and offer the opportunity for aspiring leaders to pay it forward in support of others. Success is not a competition. The competition should be empowering and mentoring someone else to reach success.

Our learning is that we need each other. Male leaders should be accountable for supporting women, yet it is also our responsibility to tackle gender inequality in the education system. Be 10% braver, and if you lack that support system or mentor, don't let that hold you back from being the person you are destined to be. Find your *community*, build your *confidence* and continuously invite other women into it. Surround yourself with a *community* that will *challenge* you, support you and cheer you on!

Passing on being 10% braver

- *Challenge* and *confidence*: search for opportunities to put yourself out there and get uncomfortable; that's how you grow. Take risks.

- *Connection, community* and *collaboration*: find your *community* and continue to make it grow. Work together. Successful women are more successful as a tribe of women, having each other's backs.

- *Challenge and confidence*: don't give up! When you do have a setback, learn from it and push forward. Don't let it stop you; see it as failing forward.

- *Clarity* and *communication*: be sure to set goals and know your intentions. Be true to yourself and those around you.

REFERENCES

Coccia, J. P. (2019) The journey to leadership: A phenomenological study of the lived experiences of six women in K-12 school administration. Doctoral dissertation. Retrieved from ProQuest Dissertations and Theses Global, Order No. 13425760.

Dana, J. and Bourisaw, D. (2006) 'Overlooked leaders', *American School Board Journal*, 193(6): 27–30.

Derks, B., Van Laar, C. and Ellemers, N. (2016) 'The queen bee phenomenon: Why women leaders distance themselves from junior women', *The Leadership Quarterly*, 27: 456–69.

Dunbar, D. P. and Kinnersley, R. T. (2011) 'Mentoring female administrators toward leadership success', *Delta Kappa Gamma Bulletin*, 77(3): 17–24.

Egri McCauley, M. (2019) A phenomenological study: Exploring female superintendents' lived experiences to understand factors related to their superintendency career paths in Pennsylvania. Doctoral dissertation. Retrieved from ProQuest Dissertations and Theses Global, Order No. 13815204.

Elias, E. (2018) 'Lessons learned from women in leadership positions', *Work*, 59(2): 175–81.

Faniko, K., Ellemers, N., Derks, B. and Lorenzi-Cioldi, F. (2017) 'Nothing *changes, really:* Why women who break the glass ceiling end up reinforcing it', *Personality and Social Psychology*, 43(5): 638–51 [Online]. Available at: doi:10.1177/0146167217695551 (accessed 1 April 2020).

National Center for Educational Statistics (NCES) (2017) Homepage [Online]. Available at: https://nces.ed.gov/# (accessed 26 December 2019).

Ragins, B. R. and Kram, K. E. (2007) *The Handbook of Mentoring at Work: Theory, Research, and Practice.* Thousand Oaks, CA: Sage.

Scharmer, C. O. (2016) *Theory U: Leading from the Future as it Emerges – The social technology of presencing.* San Francisco, CA: Berrett-Koehler.

PART 6
TACKLING AN UNFAIR SYSTEM

27

WE CAN'T BE WHAT WE CAN'T SEE: MAKE SURE YOU'RE NOT THE ONE BLOCKING THE VIEW

Penny Rabiger

KEY POINTS

This chapter outlines some of the things I have learned when:

- Organising an event;
- Calling out lack of diversity;
- Being asked to speak at an event.

INTRODUCTION

Over the past four years, my work with the Black, Asian and Minority Ethnic Educators Network (BAMEed Network, n.d.) has compelled me to act concerning the lack of diversity at many events. Being 10% braver is only half of the story; it also takes resilience to navigate any pushback, and patience to unpick the often-fragile responses to *challenge* around the highly charged issues of race, gender and representation (DiAngelo, 2018a, b).

Research by McKinsey and Company (Hunt et al., 2015) shows that having diverse voices in our organisations is great for productivity, creativity and decision making. It creates diversity of thought and action, which is a goal for any education sector event working to cater to a diverse range of attendees from a variety of contexts. I use the #WomenEd values to communicate why diversity and representation at events are important.

CLARITY

Let's be clear: despite the comfort of working with people like yourself, we achieve more with a group of people who have had different experiences from each other, including socio-economic background, race, gender, education and political outlook (Hunt et al., 2015).

#WomenEd recognises that we are socialised to assume (white) men are the best fit when it comes to speaking authoritatively. There is already a large number of white men who are authorities on a subject and are well-known, as they have been given legitimation as voices of authority (Milstein, 2014; The Royal Society, 2015). We need to break this cycle, lest we only draw on this narrow pool. This means looking beyond the usual suspects and to a more diverse range of voices, which may even be unfamiliar. Being 10% braver means pushing this vital issue with clarity, which, at times, causes discomfort for myself, for others and even necessary personal or professional sacrifice.

Tokenism is choosing someone *only* because they are from an ethnic minority group and/or a woman, choosing someone to talk without the required expertise, or who is not a good public speaker, or not qualified for the job, *just because* you need to fill a quota. This would be counterproductive as, if they were less than convincing, the cycle is further reinforced.

Balance means intentionally looking for a range of opinions, as well as a range of routes to getting there. It means thinking creatively about who is speaking and about what. We need to *challenge* carefully to include a range of voices that are not only white men.

Thinking about balance and inclusion means considering the programme contents as well as the people who speak on stage. I have had to think carefully, to research or seek out a critical friend to help me consider how to widen my and others' perspectives when planning a programme.

COMMUNITY

'Diversity is being invited to the party: Inclusion is being asked to dance!' (Myers, 2015)

We mustn't annex people in our *community* into talking only about their race, gender or other marginalised aspects of their person, unless an event directly deals with these issues and/or these are their explicitly stated areas of interest, experience and expertise.

We must ensure that people from diverse backgrounds are seen everywhere. Saying that an event is taking place in an area of the country which doesn't serve a diverse population and/or that there are no diverse teachers in that area is not acceptable. People can travel if necessary or it could be an online event which enables contributors from any geographical location. Representation doesn't mean an exact science of like for like, but a range of voices. It would, in fact, be sensible to be even more committed to diverse representation in an area where this isn't seen much, as we are prone to the white-man-bias described above, unless we actively disrupt this and provide a greater variety of voices and views.

CONNECTION AND COLLABORATION

A commonly heard excuse for events that have all-male or all-white speakers is that someone dropped out at the last minute. Organisers can start with a speaker preference list with an 'over-subscription' from typically underrepresented groups instead (Milstein, 2014).

You may find that your circle doesn't include people from diverse backgrounds. You might need to broaden your own echo-chamber of professional acquaintance, and there are ways to get help. Teacher unions, universities, The Equalities Trust, Runnymede, the BAMEed Network, #WomenEd, #DisabilityEd, #LGBTed can all help.

CONFIDENCE

It's important to make it easy for people to accept or decline an invitation to speak. I ask people to tell me about their expertise, and what they would feel confident speaking about. That way I can tell them about an event and ask if they see themselves speaking at it, should there be an opportunity to do so, without promising anything.

How events prepare their speakers, panel members and workshop facilitators is extremely important. They should feel confident, know what and who to expect, with a view to breaking down class and other cultural barriers. Knowing the dress code, or that lunch is included, is important. This can be covered easily by issuing a one-page outline of what to expect.

A good panel session will be dynamic, may include people deliberately chosen for their opposing views, and may have some controversial or provocative elements. However, care needs to be taken not to set people up for humiliation, and not to pit people against each other in a way that is unfair (Hirsch, 2019). They should know what's being discussed and who the other panel members are. Although it may lead to lively debate and good entertainment for your audience, avoid a panel title and discussion which compounds stereotypes for already marginalised people. As above, don't ever invite someone from a marginalised group to represent that group unless they want to, but do include a diverse range of voices who are experts in their field.

CHALLENGE

It's hard to decline to speak at an event because of the lack of diversity, especially if you would really like to be there. It's harder still if you see yourself replaced with someone who won't contribute to better representation. But you can help the event organisers understand why representation is needed. A part of this is being brave and principled in providing them with robust *challenge*.

It's surprising how difficult it can be to get event organisers to see why representation is needed, or why, despite good intentions, they are responsible to ensure diversity and not leave it to chance. Here are some frequent responses I've encountered that you may hear when you *challenge*.

'We're a grassroots organisation and don't have time.'

If you can't do it well, don't do it at all. Many grassroots organisations are run by people working full time in other jobs, with families, studies and other volunteer roles. In the words of Spiderman's Uncle Ben, 'with great power comes great responsibility'.

'We ask people to volunteer themselves so we can't control who comes forward.'

This is problematic if it is the only way to recruit speakers. Reach out to large organisations to help you circulate invitations by email or in their newsletters to their members.

Use a range of social media platforms, for example Twitter, LinkedIn, Facebook and Instagram, widening who will see your call for speakers. If you use a platform like Eventbrite, this will also help people to find your event.

'We can't control who attends our events.'

Having a diverse range of speakers on the programme may boost the number of people from marginalised groups that attend an event. However, many events in the education sector, especially those aimed at leadership, will see few people from BAME backgrounds in attendance. There can be reasons for this. For example, the cost of tickets and getting away from school are difficult for some people from marginalised backgrounds, especially as these will be people less likely to be in the higher-paid and more autonomous roles that allow for event attendance. A travel subsidy or early-bird rate solves this. Offering a bursary for early-career teachers or aspiring leaders from BAME backgrounds and/or other marginalised groups, alongside a statement around commitment to diversity and inclusion, can work. Some people feel uncomfortable about the prospect of being the only person of colour in a roomful of people they don't know, so group discounts are useful so that colleagues can invite someone with whom they feel comfortable. Online events offer the benefits of a wider field of both contributors and participants so are worth consideration.

'We can't pay our speakers.'

A complex system of inherent privilege means that senior, white men may be able to generously give their time to speak at your event for free. Others may find themselves less able to, without personal financial sacrifice, not only because of travel costs but also perhaps because of the fees they pay to carers for dependents whilst at your event. In many cases, a man may not be expected to take on such a role and has more available time. Data on gender and race pay gaps show why this is fact (Henehan, 2018; NEU, 2019).

(BE THE) CHANGE (AGENT)

'It's hard to be what you can't see.' (Wright Edelman, 2015)

You're not an innocent bystander; you're a *change* agent with an opportunity and a responsibility to ensure broad, balanced content and representation at any event which you attend, speak at or organise. Even if it's not your event, you don't know the organisers, or were just asked to take part or come along, you can and should take responsibility for the diversity of voices included.

If you're approached to speak, ask who else is speaking and how they came to ask you. A growing number of people do this and will politely decline to speak if there is a lack of diversity, offering instead suggestions for other people. This can be hard to do if you would like to get some exposure for yourself. However, true commitment to anti-sexist and anti-racist activism is powerful and effective; it should be the starting point for all educators. Chances are, you'll get to speak after all since your suggestions will have helped the organisers to create a better balance and your presence isn't going to be part of an identical line-up now. Leading think-tanks like the Institute for Public Policy Reform and some universities like the London School of Economics have committed to no longer holding or supporting events that feature all-white or all-male speakers and panel members. Why shouldn't we all?

REFERENCES
BAMEed Network Speakers Page (n.d.) Homepage [Online]. Available at: www.bameednetwork.com/speakers (accessed 12 October 2019).

DiAngelo, R. (2018a) 'Why "I'm not racist" is only half the story', *YouTube*, 1 October [Online]. Available at: www.youtube.com/watch?v=kzLT54QjclA&feature=youtu.be (accessed 27 September 2019).

DiAngelo, R. (2018b) 'Deconstructing white fragility', *YouTube*, 20 March. Available at: www.youtube.com/watch?v=h7mzj0cVL0Q&feature=youtu.be (accessed 27 September 2019).

Henehan, K. (2018) 'The £3.2bn pay penalty facing black and ethnic minority workers', *Resolution Foundation*, 27 December [Online]. Available at: www.resolutionfoundation.org/comment/the-3-2bn-pay-penalty-facing-black-and-ethnic-minority-workers (accessed 12 October 2019).

Hirsch, A. (2019) 'Expecting me to explain racism is exploitative – that's not my job', *The Guardian*, 22 May [Online]. Available at: www.theguardian.com/commentisfree/2019/may/22/racism-tv-debate-exploitative (accessed 11 October 2019).

Hunt, V., Layton, D. and Prince, S. (2015) 'Diversity matters', McKinsey & Co., 2 February [Online]. Available at: https://mck.co/2lvVXjd (accessed 27 September 2019).

Milstein, S. (2014) 'Putting an end to conferences dominated by white men', *Harvard Business Review*, 23 January [Online]. Available at: https://hbr.org/2014/01/theres-no-excuse-for-all-white-male-panels (accessed 27 September 2019).

Myers, V. (2015) 'Diversity is being invited to the party: Inclusion is being asked to dance', *YouTube*, 10 December [Online]. Available at: www.youtube.com/watch?v=9gS2VPUkB3M (accessed 27 September 2019).

National Education Union (NEU) (2019) 'The gender pay gap', NEU, 20 December [Online]. Available at: https://neu.org.uk/policy/gender-pay-gap (accessed 12 October 2019).

The Royal Society (2015) 'Understanding unconscious bias', *YouTube*, 17 November [Online]. Available at: www.youtube.com/watch?v=dVp9Z5k0dEE (accessed 27 September 2019).

Wright Edelman, M. (2015) 'It's hard to be what you can't see', *Children's Defense Fund*, 21 August [Online]. Available at: www.childrensdefense.org/child-watch-columns/health/2015/its-hard-to-be-what-you-cant-see (accessed 27 September 2019).

28

WHAT TO DO IF YOU FIND YOURSELF WORKING FOR A BULLY

Beatus Magistra

KEY POINTS

Why did I need to be 10% braver?

- I was spoken to in a way which was not acceptable more than once. At first, it was easy to dismiss my reaction as oversensitivity on my part, as a misunderstanding, a difference in temperament. After a while, incidents became more pointed.
- Other people were also being bullied... it was happening because there was a bully.
- Because maintaining silence is giving permission. Doing nothing about the situation was sending the message that bullying behaviour is acceptable and accepted.

INTRODUCTION

Bullying. When I embarked upon a career *change* to become a teacher, bullying was an area about which I felt confident. I could define and describe bullying in my sleep. Despite this, I had not understood the *challenges* specific to responding to bullying between children in school, I had not realised that dealing with bullying between children I was responsible for and cared about would be different, both practically and emotionally, from dealing with bullying of anonymised children whom I did not know. I had certainly not expected to encounter bullying of teachers by school leaders.

WHAT DID BEING 10% BRAVER LOOK LIKE FOR ME?

Being 10% braver looked like speaking candidly to others about what I was experiencing, about things that had happened, how I felt and what I was doing. In this case, saying nothing in my own defence would send the message that it was acceptable to bully me. I told colleagues that I had been given a support plan. I told them that there was no informal support provided beforehand. I said that the targets didn't make sense and that I had been told they couldn't be removed from the plan, even though it was clear that they were not appropriate. I explained that I was told my planning was inadequate in the same week as I was asked to support a colleague with their planning. I said that 'students' books' was a target, yet the feedback I received on my students' books was almost all positive and the point for improvement was not to allow any pictures or story maps to be drawn directly on to lined paper.

I shared that I had been shouted at, that I had been 'shushed' in front of children, that a finger had been wagged in my face on more than one occasion. I shared my emotional response, that I cried most days, that I felt sick coming to work, and I discussed the practical steps that I was taking, that I had spoken to my union and emailed governors. This was often uncomfortable and left me feeling vulnerable with colleagues I had not known for long.

One day, someone asked how I was managing to speak so openly. I explained that it was a conscious choice to do so, that it was uncomfortable but that I was trying to rise to the *challenge* for two reasons: first because I was doing nothing wrong, I wasn't being treated badly as a consequence of something negative I had done. It was not happening because I deserved it. Keeping quiet added to the sense of shame and self-blame. Choosing to speak, to say 'bullying' aloud, to say, 'It's not OK' reminded me of those truths. Second, I explained that if this was being done to me, I felt it likely that it was being done to others. Research into school bullying tells us that having a friend is a protective factor against being a victim of bullying (Perry et al. 2001). If someone else was going through the same thing and they knew about my experience, then perhaps they wouldn't blame themselves, perhaps they wouldn't feel alone.

For me, being 10% braver looked like contacting my union and asking for help. It looked like enduring uncomfortable meetings, making myself say to governors that my practice was not improving because of 'support', that the issue wasn't my practice, that 'support' didn't involve any actual support.

Iesha Small's book, *The Unexpected Leader* (2019: 3) contains some words of wisdom which feel very personal: 'know what makes you different; find out how to use it as a strength; find others who see it as a strength; use your uniqueness to add value.'

BULLYING AT WORK

Whitney and Smith (1993: 7) clarify that it is not bullying when two young people 'of about the same strength have the odd fight or quarrel'. The key aspects of their definition (repetition and power imbalance) are also found in definitions of bullying in other circumstances: in the workplace (e.g. Hoel and Cooper, 2001; Tehrani, 2001), and between older adults in residential settings (Monks and Mahdavi, 2013).

As teachers, we are a self-reflective lot. We work hard, not because of the extrinsic motivation of salary but because we crave the lightbulb moments, the success of our pupils and the knowledge that we have played our part in the sculpting of future doctors, nurses, artists, engineers and construction workers. We build and nurture connections with pupils, working together with colleagues, always seeking to use past successes and *challenges* to inform and hone current practice. The success of teachers encompasses the academic but can also include showing young people how to respond to challenging situations with peers, how to show kindness and compassion. We are so much more than the facilitators of knowledge transfer and yet we can struggle to defend ourselves in the determined way we stand up for those whom we teach. So why is identifying and responding to bullying that happens to teachers so challenging? The key is an imbalance of power. It is an imbalance which is part of our daily working life, which is part of a hierarchical structure that can include many levels. Further difficulties can be exacerbated by grievance policies which remind the reader to be sure they don't mistake strong leadership for bullying. These aspects can further erode the *confidence* to believe in ourselves and to act on the knowledge that it's not acceptable for teachers to be bullied.

ATTACKING VALUES

Bullying erodes community

When a teacher is bullied, it can isolate them from their colleagues. When a teacher sees a colleague being bullied, it can be very difficult to speak up for them and risk becoming isolated as well. Teachers are parents, spouses, mortgage and rent payers with financial responsibilities. The perceived risk of aligning oneself with a colleague who is experiencing bullying is huge. The worries are real. What if I am next? What would I do? Even if I move on, I need a reference.

Bullying obliterates connection

Bullying behaviour, especially from someone in a leadership role, damages people in a variety of ways. Bullying erodes our sense of joy, the euphoria that comes with knowing we are doing the best job we can for our pupils. Bullying devastates the self-worth and self-esteem of individuals, but, beyond that, it attacks a *connection* that should exist and provide support between existing and aspiring leaders – how could someone celebrate the *connection* with a leader who bullies others?

Bullying undermines collaboration

Collaboration is eroded by working in an environment controlled by bullies. When someone is bullied, it is challenging for them to share their experiences with others, and even more challenging to find positive points of view to share. As with *community*, the risks of collaborating with a colleague who is being bullied can seem great. As the person being bullied, asking a colleague to go out on a limb and collaborate with you can feel unfair.

Bullying annihilates communication

Good *communication* is based on trust and is destroyed when bullying is involved. Bullying has such a negative influence on so many of our shared values and affects *communication*; if we can't share ideas, it's hard to share values. If our sense of *community* is damaged, it's harder to focus on common ideals. If the *connection* between existing and aspiring leaders is lost, a key method of sharing and promoting the vision is gone.

The words of others do not define you

I remember saying this on numerous occasions to children in my class or in the playground. Insulting, *confidence*-crushing things are horrible to hear, but, in the moments of strength between the self-doubt, remember – the words of another do not have the power to make you something that you are not. The words and opinions of another do not have the power to *change* the opinions of the rest of your *community*, nor the rest of the world, although it may feel like that.

Bullying is not acceptable

This may need to be a mantra that you repeat, aloud or silently, to remind yourself of this fact. There is no circumstance in which bullying can be tolerated. It is not acceptable for a colleague, line manager, headteacher or fellow professional to bully you. Do not accept it. It is unacceptable.

To end on a word of hope: I left when I was ready to no longer be a teacher. A rest was, as it turned out, better than a *change*. I have a new role in a new school with leadership and colleagues who indeed do value the things about me which are unique. I was 10% braver and the outcome was fantastic.

Passing on being 10% braver

- Keep a record of things that have been said or done. This will enable others to help and support you and will remind you that the problem is serious, continuing and not going away. It might help you to see the need to seek help.

- Contact your union; follow their advice. They are likely to want different policies as well as details of what has happened. This doesn't mean they don't believe you; it helps them to do their job.

- Talk. Don't hide away. Find someone you trust and speak to them. Maintaining a human *connection* with others will stop you from being isolated and remind you that you are valuable, important, unique and many other things.

- Build a support network and allow it to support you. Friends, colleagues and family members can all be part of the net that keeps you from falling. Additionally, organisations such as the Education Support Partnership are there to provide mental health and wellbeing support to people working in education, including a 24-hour telephone helpline (0800 056 2561).

- I feel strongly that the answer is to offer help and support. Whether you stand with the person so they feel less alone, or whether you are able to stand up for them in a more obvious way, remember the words of Desmond Tutu: 'If you are neutral in situations of injustice, you have chosen the side of the oppressor.'

REFERENCES

Hoel, H. and Cooper, C. L. (2001) 'Origins of bullying: Theoretical frameworks for explaining workplace bullying', in N. Tehrani (ed.), *Building a Culture of Respect: Managing Bullying at Work*. London/New York: Taylor & Francis, pp. 3–19.

Monks, C. P. and Mahdavi, J. A. (2013) Bullying between residents in residential care settings for older adults. Unpublished research report.

Perry, D. G., Hodges, E. V. E. and Egan, S. K. (2001) 'Determinants of chronic victimization by peers: A review and new model of family influence', in J. Juvonen and S. Graham (eds), *Peer Harassment in School: The Plight of the Vulnerable and Victimized*. New York: The Guilford Press, pp. 73–104.

Small, I. (2019) *The Unexpected Leader*. Camarthen: Independent Thinking Press.

Tehrani, N. (ed.) (2001) *Building a Culture of Respect: Managing Bullying at Work.* London/New York: Taylor & Francis.

Whitney, I. and Smith, P. K. (1993) 'A survey of the nature and extent of bullying in junior/middle and secondary schools', *Educational Research, 35* (1): 3-25.

29

PREGNANT AND SCREWED

Hannah Dalton and Kiran Mahil

KEY POINTS

The authors of this chapter were middle leaders who were pregnant at the same time. They had to become 10% braver for these reasons:

- Poisonous presumptions – it felt as though colleagues were coming to the conclusion that we couldn't possibly be interested in developing our careers, on becoming pregnant;
- Blaze that trail – there was nobody, in our setting, modelling what motherhood and leadership looked like. We had to prove to ourselves, and for other colleagues, that it can be done;
- Our daughters and yours – we believe it's important to show our girls that you can be whoever you want to be;
- For teachers everywhere – we want to create a new way of working that benefits everyone in schools.

INTRODUCTION

Given that teaching was one of the first jobs women were allowed to do, it is shocking that there still remain so many barriers for women to succeed in schools today. The reality of the situation is that this worsens when you have children. The Institute for Fiscal Studies reported that, by the age of 42, mothers who are in full-time work are earning 11% less than full-time women without children (Costa Dias et al., 2016). The joint Department for Business, Innovation and Skills and Equality and Human Rights Commission research into pregnancy and maternity discrimination found that 20% of working mums said they had experienced harassment or negative comments related to pregnancy or flexible working from their employer and/or colleagues (2016). Whilst there has been no substantial school sector study into the motherhood penalty, in August 2019 *tes* reported growing fears that schools are discriminating against pregnant teachers (Speck, 2019).

We have both felt that, after having children of our own, there was an assumption by management that we were no longer able to educate, or were interested in educating, anybody's children. From our personal experiences and those of countless other teacher mums we've talked to, this is far from the truth. For many of us, our jobs can matter even more on becoming a parent. We are suddenly now responsible, in our professional and personal lives, for nurturing the citizens we become and the communities of which we are a part.

So, why did we discover so many stories of women being devalued when pregnant and demoted and downtrodden on return? The system is not designed to support women through this vital process and there are not enough enlightened leaders willing to do anything about it. It is incumbent on all of us to *change* it, at every level in which we operate. By reflecting on personal experience and exploring professional best practice, this chapter outlines practical steps that can be taken to improve schools as workplaces for parents.

PREGNANT BODIES

It should not be forgotten that women's bodies go through significant physiological *change*s during pregnancy. This is why great medical attention and care are required during this period. Expectant mothers have a legal right to paid antenatal care. This extends to antenatal or parenting classes recommended by a doctor and a midwife. For some women, the strain of pregnancy can take its toll and sickness in pregnancy is a reality for many expectant mothers. Normal sickness procedures should be followed during pregnancy as pregnant employees have the same right to paid sick leave as any other employee. However, the school must record any pregnancy-related absence separately from other sick leave, so that this is not used to the employee's disadvantage.

It is worth checking how HR has recorded your absence, and we would strongly encourage any reader who feels as though their legal rights have not been met to get in contact with a trade union representative who can negotiate on your behalf.

HOW SHOULD YOU BE TREATED WHEN PREGNANT?

The key to understanding how to treat a pregnant woman is to remember that she is an individual. Pregnancy can be a long and complex journey for some, and for others less so. There need to be clear lines of *communication* and frequent check-ins to enquire how the expectant mother is managing, both physically and mentally, with her changing body. An approach which might have no effect on a woman at three months' pregnant may be too much at eight months.

For example, Kiran was assigned to run an end-of-term trip with the whole of Year 7 to a castle. This was far from an ideal situation. The onus should not be on the expectant mother to ask whether that can be *change*d. We would argue that leadership teams should expect to make reasonable adjustments, particularly if the legally required risk assessment has identified any risk to the employee or their baby. We feel that progressive leadership teams should be prepared to relax expectations of movement between classrooms, the amount of teaching on any one day, how many late nights are really required in any one week and how many duties are done around school. Again, the key here is that any adaptions to the working week of pregnant teachers must be done in *collaboration* with them. Our mantra is that approaches must be designed with you and not done to you.

Expectant mothers should expect to be asked their views on what they want to happen when on maternity leave. Hannah wrote a document for her replacement on 'absolute priorities' which she wanted to be addressed when she was away from the role, and then on aspects of the role which she was happy for the maternity cover to make her own. It was important to Hannah that she would not have to restart everything she had worked hard to put in place when she returned to school.

HOW SHOULD YOU BE TREATED WHEN ON MATERNITY LEAVE?

There should be a discussion with the expectant mother and her line manager (or HR) before she begins her maternity leave, with regards to her expectations about *communication* whilst on leave. Although feelings and circumstances can *change* once the baby has arrived, those on maternity leave should be able to set out whether they want to be informed of *changes* in policy or new positions being advertised, and whether they intend to use their 'keeping in touch' (KIT) days. Kiran wanted to keep *communication* lines open during her maternity leave. It was what allowed her to apply for promoted posts on both of her maternity leaves, one of which was successful, so it can be done. Of course, those on maternity leave have every right to ask for minimal *communication* too. Again, the power should lie with the woman on maternity leave when deciding how much contact there is with work.

There are ways in which a school can make those on maternity leave feel valued and still a part of the school *community*. If there is a staff social society, you should still be invited to non-working events, and many schools invite new mothers in with their baby to conduct meetings or to arrange KIT days. If there isn't such a society and those on maternity leave want to be kept up to date with social events, perhaps asking a friend to send out plans would be useful.

Maternity leave can be a time for career development, too. The Maternity Teacher Paternity Teacher (MTPT) project offers men and women on leave the chance to engage in real CPD with coaching, allowing you to maintain your teacher identity whilst on leave and to connect with existing and aspiring leaders (see www.mtpt.org. uk). The project also hosts coffee mornings to enable you to build your *community* outside of your school setting. Both of us felt the need to pursue our own professional development whilst on leave and so we sought out opportunities that worked with our family schedules. Kiran undertook textbook material writing and Hannah attended curriculum leadership courses whilst on leave. We both found that engaging in professional development whilst we were on maternity leave gave us *confidence* about returning.

HOW SHOULD YOU BE TREATED ON RETURN FROM MATERNITY LEAVE?

Returning to work can be a challenging time for many mothers – it's perfectly normal to experience some anxiety about leaving your baby or about your ability to manage your job as well as you did before. This makes a full induction on return absolutely essential; you need to feel confident that you can do your job again. Expectant mothers should expect to receive key updates from their headteacher, their department area, on any *changes* to the team they are re-joining, to be briefed about any important curriculum developments and be given up-to-date logins, keys, and so on. You should indicate that you expect these things when you arrange your return date with the headteacher as not all schools have the forethought to consider how much you might have missed.

You should also be asked if you have any breastfeeding needs so that a room can be set aside for you. We've heard stories of women struggling in toilet cubicles with pumping; this is simply unfair. We believe your induction should be a week or two, so you are given time to bring yourself back up to speed. If it feels it's getting too much, you must raise the issues with your line manager. It is incumbent on the school to find a way through for all parties. You need clarity on the roles and responsibilities to which you are returning, which is particularly important if you are returning part time. Part-time work should not result in part pay for the same job; too many women have surrendered their leadership positions because they were being asked to carry out the same role they had before, in fewer hours.

HOW CAN YOU MAKE IT WORK FOR YOU?

We asked the #WomenEd *community* on Twitter for strategies from women who have successfully navigated having children and leading in schools. We were overwhelmed by the generosity, openness and strength of the response we got. The key messages from those who are not only surviving but thriving being mothers and leaders are as follows:

- There is no 'right' way – every one of us is an individual with unique circumstances. We have heard from many women who have returned both full and part time – each had to make their situation work for them and their family, to find the right balance. You have to do what is right for you and there is no hierarchy of success.
- Be kind to yourself – try to carve out some 'me' time. For Hannah, it was one day during every half term where she visited an art gallery on her own, just for her.

Other women have joined a choir, joined a gym or have an hour to themselves reading after their little ones have gone to bed. You need to treat yourself occasionally and these little things will keep you going when the going gets tough.

- Decide on your non-negotiables – there are some things that you will not let go of; it might be getting home for bedtime stories and having photocopying done before you leave work. Other things have to slide occasionally, and that's OK.
- Don't be afraid to ask for help – you will inevitably need it at some point! Being a successful leader and mother does not mean managing everything on your own.
- Guilt is a wasted emotion – and only harms you. Be realistic and transparent about what you can and cannot do, and colleagues will respect you for it.

We took the deliberate decision to collaborate with women leaders when writing this chapter as there are many different ways to make pregnancy, parenting and professional growth work for you. We have found these words of advice have become our everyday affirmations. We hope you find inspiration in them too.

Passing on being 10% braver

- Know your worth - becoming a parent adds to your power, wealth of talents, experience and skills. It can give you a new perspective on work-related issues. Parenting and teaching is double the difference. Own this as an advantage, because you are amazing.
- Use your voice - if it feels as though how you're being treated is not acceptable, it usually isn't. Call it out and *challenge* the status quo if you need to. Try to get others to amplify your voice too.
- Find your tribe - whether it be in a trade union, colleagues at work or the #WomenEd *community*. There is real strength in drawing support from others.
- Have your cake and eat it. Don't settle for the crumbs - combining work and parenting isn't a luxury for many of us. It's a necessity. And it should not result in financial loss. Be prepared to persist for proper pay.
- If we didn't have children, none of us would have jobs - a helpful reminder to us all.

REFERENCES

Costa Dias, M., Elming, W. and Joyce, R. (2016) 'The gender wage gap', The Institute of Fiscal Studies [Online]. Available at: www.ifs.org.uk/publications/84 (accessed 25 October 2019).

Department for Business, Innovation and Skills (BIS) and the Equality and Human Rights Commission (2016) Pregnancy and Maternity Related Discrimination and Disadvantage: Experience of Mothers. Available at: www.equalityhumanrights.com/en/managing-pregnancy-and-maternity-workplace/pregnancy-and-maternity-discrimination-research-findings (accessed 25 October 2019).

Speck, D. (2019) 'Are schools discriminating against pregnant teachers?', tes, 1 August [Online]. Available at: www.tes.com/news/are-schools-discriminating-against-pregnant-teachers (accessed 25 October 2019).

30
DEALING WITH THE MOTHERHOOD PENALTY AS A LEADER

Naomi Shenton

KEY POINTS

This chapter will:

- Explore how I negotiated part-time working when applying for a job advertised as full time;
- Outline how I applied for, and secured, a senior leadership role as a mother of a toddler;
- Explain how I applied for, and secured, a multi-academy trust-wide role whilst pregnant.

INTRODUCTION

Clarity is crucial to acknowledging and addressing the imbalance in leadership. However, we must be careful not to conflate the terms mother and woman, and there is more research about the latter than the former. We do know that, despite 74% of teachers being female, only 65% of headteachers are female, and this drops significantly to 36% at secondary level (Vaughan, 2015). In 2004, Coleman found that only 60% of female headteachers were mothers, whereas 90% of male headteachers were fathers (Coleman, 2005).

UNDERSTANDING SOCIETAL EXPECTATIONS

In December 2017, assistant principal roles were advertised at my school. I applied and was successful, as was a male colleague, who, like me, had a 1-year-old daughter and planned to have more children in the future. Many well-meaning friends and colleagues questioned how I was going to balance the pressures of family and leadership, and suggested that I had sacrificed having more children. No one asked my male colleague these questions. Both of us now have two daughters and successfully balance family life and work, but the societal pressures and expectations that we face differ. I believe it is important that mother-leaders share their stories to *challenge* stereotypes, provide positive role models and empower other women to lead.

SELF-PERCEPTION

Society continues to expect women to be the primary carers for children; Woodhouse (2016) calls this the 'socially expected decision'. This is illustrated perfectly by colleagues' responses to my promotion as they assumed that, as a woman, I was primarily responsible for childcare. A fellow mother-teacher, only half-jokingly, declared that I was mad when hearing of my promotion, and I am often asked who is looking after the children. As mothers, we can feel bombarded by this message from the media and in our day-to-day interactions.

This can have a strong impact on our own self-perceptions of motherhood and may limit women's leadership (Woodhouse, 2016). Again, this is echoed in my personal experience; despite wanting the role and believing I could be successful, I listened to the voices around me and nearly did not apply for promotion, as I worried it would prevent me from being a good mother. This is a significant concern in education, with Kell's research finding an 'undeniable gulf' in the career progression of mothers and fathers. More than 80% of her mother-participants referred to the negative impact of parenthood on their career aspirations (Kell, 2016: 166).

Society's view of mothers as carers is so ingrained that women make decisions which are detrimental to their careers in preparation for motherhood – in Sandberg's terminology, you 'leave before you leave' (2013: 92). The assumption that mothers are, or should be, primary carers is even more disturbing when held by those in school leadership or governance. Coleman's research found that mothers were discriminated against in recruitment processes, with some interview panels showing concern about how women were going to balance their family and leadership responsibilities (Coleman, 2005). This research is now dated, however anecdotal evidence shared within the #WomenEd *community* suggests that these attitudes persist in some leadership teams.

CONNECTION

We must consistently *challenge* societal expectations to overturn this disparity in aspirations, encourage more women to have the *confidence* to be 10% braver and ensure that we have more mother-leaders. Lincoln (2016) explained that an increased visibility of women in senior roles demonstrates the possibility of career progression to other women, and I would argue that the same effect is true when dealing specifically with mothers. As Wilson noted, *community* is important in enabling 'women leaders to be connected and supported' (2019: 7).

The MTPT Project, @maternityCPD, is a *community* of mothers, and fathers, who are teachers and leaders (see www.mtpt.org.uk/research). The *community*'s significant online presence increases the visibility, and therefore normality, of ambitious, career-driven parents, whilst also providing much needed *connection* and support. On Twitter,

I discovered a host of mother-leaders, something which I had struggled to find offline and which confirmed for me that motherhood and leadership can be compatible.

OVERCOMING PRACTICAL HURDLES: PREGNANCY

Pregnancy itself can have an impact on career progression. Whilst in the early stages of pregnancy, an additional trust-wide role was advertised by my employer. I was torn – the role seemed perfect, but the timing awful. It was only after my principal emphasised that I should not let pregnancy impede me that I had the *confidence* to apply and was then successful. Sandberg takes this further by initiating conversations about motherhood with women who are not pregnant but seem to be hesitating in their careers. Her experience of these conversations is overwhelmingly positive; however, she acknowledges the potential legal ramifications and always gives women the option not to respond. Crucially, she makes it explicit that she does not want women 'limiting their options unnecessarily' (Sandberg, 2013: 96).

As a mother-headteacher, Rebecca Cramer also believes that it is important to communicate openly about family plans, explaining that her 'staff know that there are no barriers at work to them having children' (Maternity CPD, 2018a). If we can disseminate this attitude across the education system, then we have the power to make significant *change* and, indeed, to overcome the motherhood penalty for ourselves and the generations that follow.

OVERCOMING PRACTICAL HURDLES: PARENTAL LEAVE

Research suggests that career breaks following the birth of children contribute to the gender inequality in educational leadership (Guihen, 2017: 28). Shared parental leave was introduced in the United Kingdom in 2015, with the aim of reducing this inequality, however by 2019 only 2% of families were using it. Shared parental leave is often not remunerated in line with maternity pay and many 'workplaces haven't caught up' (Usborne, 2019).

By ensuring that our schools and trusts produce and promote appropriate shared parental leave policies, we can have an impact on both women and men as they juggle parenthood and careers. However, maternity leave does not need to stall career progression. When my eldest daughter was born in 2016, I felt conflicted. I loved spending time with her, however I felt obliged to be cut off from the career which had driven me all my adult life and this left me somewhat adrift. By 2019, when my second daughter was born, I had connected with networks of mother-teachers and leaders and felt empowered to make maternity leave work for me, which included using KIT time flexibly and my daughter accompanying me to meetings. This was significant both for ease of breastfeeding and because I acted as a role model, signalling to both staff and students that motherhood and leadership are not mutually exclusive.

OVERCOMING PRACTICAL HURDLES: CHILDCARE

In an equal society, childcare should be the responsibility of all parents and therefore not contribute to the motherhood penalty in leadership. In Guihen's (2017) research into female deputy headteachers, caregiving was divided into three categories: mother as primary caregiver, mother sharing parental responsibilities with the father, and father as primary caregiver. Headteacher Kanchana Gamage shares the responsibilities of parenting with her husband, allowing both parents to be fulfilled personally and professionally (Maternity CPD, 2018b). Guihen (2017) found that, for some mother-senior leaders, their family dynamic *changed* over time, and introduced the idea of a continuum, with stay-at-home mother at one end and stay-at-home father at the other. This is the model that best describes my family, as each of us has had periods of taking primary responsibility for childcare and we have both worked part time. My parents also support with childcare. This flexibility enables us to be models of equality for our daughters as well as overcoming the financial limitations of the primary breadwinner taking maternity leave.

However careful our childcare plans, the reality is that children can get ill or have problems settling, and these are the times when mother-leaders really feel under pressure and guilt can creep in. When our eldest had chicken pox, my husband and I took turns to look after her and initially I felt guilty about doing this; however, as Cramer points out, 'the world keeps turning' (Maternity CPD, 2018a). Headteacher Angie Browne (2017) advocates clear *communication* about childcare and explaining to those around you when you are having difficulties, which I think is crucial to overcoming the motherhood penalty, both in our individual careers and by acting as role models to those around us.

FAMILY-FRIENDLY SCHOOLS

School communities have significant power to drive *change* by becoming more family friendly. There are excellent examples of schools providing on-site childcare. One teacher in south-west England told me that the onsite nursery which her son attends saved her work–life balance. Benefits for teachers can include term-time-only contracts, discounted fees or guaranteed places, as well as the physical proximity of having their children on site.

As Kell (2016) acknowledges, this provision has financial and bureaucratic complexities, however there are also many simpler steps which schools can take to become more family friendly and empower women to be mothers and leaders. Since becoming a mother, I have worked as a leader both part time and full time, depending on what has been best for my family. It is important that we provide opportunities for leaders to work part time, and for parents, both mothers and fathers, to retain their responsibilities whilst reducing their hours if they choose to. As part of a package of family-friendly measures and with strong *communication*, this can empower mothers to lead.

Passing on being 10% braver

- Connect with like-minded people virtually or in person. Twitter is a brilliant place to start, or attend regional, national or online #WomenEd events or an MTPT Project coffee morning.
- Keep communicating, whether that be about plans for future children, pregnancy and parental leave or childcare struggles.
- Embrace opportunity. If you want something, be that a promotion, flexible working or to speak at a conference, go for it. Don't let motherhood, or planned motherhood, stop you.
- Be inspired by mother-leaders and remember that you too are an inspiration to others in your circle, not least your children.

REFERENCES

Browne, A. (2017) Mama Headteacher – Juggling Childcare [Online]. Available at: www.youtube.com/watch?v=K5-baPotYQU&feature=youtu.be (accessed 30 October 2019).

Coleman, M. (2005) Gender and Headship in the Twenty-first Century [Online]. Available at: https://core.ac.uk/download/pdf/83249.pdf (accessed 26 August 2019).

Guihen, L. (2017) The Career Histories and Professional Aspirations of Women Deputy Headteachers: An Interpretative Phenomenological Analysis [Online]. Available at: https://lra.le.ac.uk/bitstream/2381/39456/1/2017guihenlphd.pdf (accessed 30 October 2019).

Kell, E. L. (2016) Shifting Identities: A Mixed-Methods Study of the Experiences of Teachers who are also Parents. Other thesis, Middlesex University [Online]. Available at: http://eprints.mdx.ac.uk/20805/1/EKellThesis.pdf (accessed 26 August 2019).

Lincoln, J. (2016) 'The perfect role model doesn't exist: We need visibility and cultural *change*', The Guardian, 12 January [Online]. Available at: www.theguardian.com/

women-in-leadership/2016/jan/12/the-perfect-role-model-doesnt-exist-we-need-visibility-and-cultural-change (accessed 26 August 2019).

Maternity CPD (2018a) Bex Cramer: Motherhood and Headship Series [Online]. Available at: www.mtpt.org.uk/motherhood-and-headship/bex-cramer-motherhood-and-headship-series (accessed 30 October 2019).

Maternity CPD (2018b) Kanchana Gamage: Motherhood and Headship Series [Online]. Available at: www.mtpt.org.uk/motherhood-and-headship/kanchana-gamage-motherhood-and-headship-series (accessed 30 October 2019).

Sandberg, S. (2013) *Lean In*. New York: Alfred A. Knopf.

Usborne, S. (2019) '"It was seen as weird": Why are so few men taking shared parental leave?', *The Guardian*, 5 October [Online]. Available at: www.theguardian.com/lifeandstyle/2019/oct/05/shared-parental-leave-seen-as-weird-paternity-leave-in-decline?CMP=Share_iOSApp_Other (accessed 30 October 2019).

Vaughan, R. (2015) 'More than 1,700 female headteachers "missing" from England's schools, says research', *tes*, 8 February. Available at: www.tes.com/news/more-1700-female-headteachers-missing-englands-schools-says-research (accessed 12 July 2020).

Wilson, H. (2019) '#WomenEd: Our story and values', in V. Porritt and K. Featherstone (eds), *10% Braver: Inspiring Women to Lead Education*. London: Sage, pp. 1–15.

Woodhouse, J. (2016) 'Motherhood, career and leadership: Time to re-think the gender binary?', British Educational Research Association blog, 29 September [Online]. Available at: www.bera.ac.uk/blog/motherhood-career-and-leadership-time-to-re-think-the-gender-binary (accessed 26 August 2019).

31
TIME TO SAY GOODBYE
Bukky Yusuf

KEY POINTS

This chapter will:

- Share the importance of knowing myself in order to gain the *confidence* to be 10% braver;
- Share the impact on myself and others when I was not being 10% braver;
- Highlight lessons I learnt in being 10% braver when it felt impossible to do so.

INTRODUCTION

'Growth is painful. *Change* is painful. But nothing is as painful as staying stuck somewhere you don't belong.' (cited in Oppong, 2017, paragraph 4)

It took me 18 months to realise, learn and accept *one* thing:

The school and I *simply* did not fit.

I had to be honest and brave enough to admit this to myself.

I had to be honest and brave enough to have conversations explaining why I planned to leave.

I had to be honest and brave enough to act and find a school where I would be a better fit.

WHY I TOOK THE ROLE

During the time spent looking for and securing my next leadership role, I was doing supply work within inner-city school science departments. The timescale was longer than I had anticipated and along the way I unsuccessfully applied to a number of schools for roles that would allow me to be a senior leader. Out of all these applications, there were only really two that I was pinning my hopes on; the others were no doubt good opportunities but, hand on heart, I was more interested in snagging the leadership role rather than paying due diligence to whether or not I was the right fit for the school.

Then I heard of a school through two different sources, sources that I trusted to know me and the type of school that would suit me as a leader. Subsequent phone calls and school visits took place, which helped me to get to know the school and the particular role a little better. With hindsight, I can see that a number of assumptions were made about what type of leader I was perceived to be, and therefore the type of schools I should work in.

At that time in my life, I was at a point where I would grab any opportunities that presented themselves. I had rightly anticipated this new role to be hard work, a *challenge*, and to demand a lot of myself to move my area of responsibility forward. I had heard a lot of positive things about the headteacher; I was very excited to be working with her. However, the expectations placed on my shoulders were wholly unrealistic, i.e. 80% grade 5+ in the first sitting on a new GCSE specification – an increase of approximately 25% from the previous year. Being keen to prove myself, I did not *challenge* these expectations.

Looking back, I can see how naïve I was. I also believe that everything happens for a reason. Thus, my chapter is dedicated to outlining signs I should have noted, the negative impact, what I learnt and some take-away advice to avoid ending up in a similar position.

THE SIGNS

Several signs highlighted the fact that not *everything* in the school was as well as it should be, such as:

- I did not meet anyone within the department during my school visit or interview (indicating that meeting the department would deter me from taking the role);
- I was given the wrong class data for my interview lesson, with a set 3 of 3 teaching group (indicating that things were not well organised);
- I was not given anything to eat during my interview (indicating a lack of care and hospitability).

Once I started in the school, these signs became flashing neon lights. I found historic issues and practices which had never been *challenge*d, yet suddenly these were things I was blamed for. These included new GCSE schemes not being in place (at interview, I was told they were being developed), a fractious department and students not engaging with the subject. When things got really challenging, I sought union advice to clarify my options and to check whether I was right to feel concerned about how things were panning out.

I was really grateful for the clear, patient and non-judgemental guidance that was provided. I learnt that as soon as you, as a professional, recognise there are issues, do seek external union advice, even if it's only to talk over what you are going through. When I finally contacted my union, the advisor explained that I should have done so earlier because doing so long after the initial issue arose placed me in a weaker position. They talked me through what the institution could do and what it would mean for me. This helped me to know which options were open to me and what I could say or do in each situation.

Fortunately for me, I was provided with support from the school which helped to turn some aspects around, as I stayed on.

LESSONS LEARNT

Despite what many of us think when we excitedly start a new role in a new school, you always know when something is not quite working out as it should. Deciding to walk away is not necessarily career damaging. If there's a huge difference between what you expected and the reality of what you experience, you are within your rights to *change* your mind.

Before this role, I had a 'tough it out to the end, no matter what' attitude. Isn't that what is best for the students? And, whilst I still do believe that we should do as much as we can for our students and that challenging experiences can help us to grow, I will no longer believe in sticking with something which clearly does not work for me. I should have asked more questions, listened to different perspectives and sought out the experiences of people who had worked there before I arrived.

THE NEGATIVE IMPACT

When I started the role, I gave myself two years to make a difference, but my bosses expected me to make a difference within one year. I walked into a situation where there were no schemes of work or lesson plans in place for the revised Key Stage 4 and Key Stage 5 curricula. However, when I started, I was not completely aware of the significant issues that would hamper the successes I had in mind.

Looking back, I remember the surreal feeling that, no matter what prior experience I had, how hard I worked (the hardest I had ever worked in my life, and I am a hard worker) or how many hours I was putting in, nothing seemed to make a difference. Additionally, the number of issues I was being pulled up for was unrelenting; for example, negative feedback from a learning walk, behaviour issues within lessons, the non-compliance of some staff. I couldn't improve everything overnight.

Over time, I was made to feel that I was not good enough. This is not to say that I made no mistakes; in some instances, with so many things which needed to be done at once, there wasn't always time to do things as well as I wanted. Once the first half-term 'honeymoon' period was over, very few of the positive things I was doing were noted by senior leaders. It led me to lose *confidence* and become very unhappy. I was not enjoying the role and wondered what I could do besides walking away. Ironically, I later found out that my predecessors had done just that – walked away.

The light at the end of the tunnel came in the form of a friend who did the same role and who understood the unique dynamics within the place we worked. They helped me navigate some of the difficulties that I was experiencing and supported me to realise that, even though I was frequently being pulled up on things, I was not always at fault.

WHAT I LEARNT

The main 'Who Moved My Cheese?' principle (Johnson, 1998) is that when the 'cheese' (i.e. my role) no longer tastes as good as it did at the start, this is a clear indicator that it's time to move on. What initially held me back from exploring other opportunities was the fear of failing that I had to overcome in order to leave a place which negated my own sense of wellbeing.

I learnt that just because things weren't working out for me and in the way I had intended, it didn't mean that all those I reported to were 'bad' people. It was clear to see that there were a number of issues in terms of strategic leadership, effective evaluation and decisions made as knee-jerk reactions. Yet, I was fortunate to find a small supportive circle of people within the school who had integrity and who helped me to experience positive moments; within supportive communities, there is always hope.

Soon after I gave my notice to resign, my headteacher (who had been incredibly supportive) advised me to find something I love to do and that matched my skill set. I will be forever grateful for this essential reminder to avoid placing myself in a square hole, based upon the fact that it is what I should be doing as part of my career.

This whole experience helped shape me into the person and leader that I am today. Most importantly, it enabled me to truly empathise with educators who experience toxic school environments. It taught me that, unless you experience it first hand, you have no idea what it feels like and of the catastrophic impact it can have upon your mind, body and soul.

I texted a friend the day I left to say that I had walked out of the school building for the last time. Their brief reply: 'Now you are safe', has stuck with me.

Passing on being 10% braver

- Be brave to identify your core values: if you are considering a leadership role, it is essential to identify your own core values (Yusuf, 2017) and what motivates you. During the summer break, I took the chance to identify what motivates me. An analysis of my top three motivators made it clear why working at that school was always going to be a *challenge*. Therefore, invest time to explore thoroughly how your core values and motivators match the core values of the school you are considering. During your school visit/tour, ask for examples that exemplify the espoused values from anyone you meet. Their responses will tell you a lot about the school.

- Be brave enough to ask the questions that matter most to you, i.e. what are the most important things for you in a school? It is a worthwhile endeavour to identify and create your own checklist.

- Be brave enough to go for what works best for you. Avoid settling.

- Be 10% braver and walk away when you have to.

I will close with some words of advice shared when Iesha Small was interviewed (in The Sizzle Podcast, 2019):

> Sometimes the place is not right for you. No shame in saying it's not the right kind of environment and that you need to move on. We need to know which types of environment we would thrive in.

REFERENCES

Johnson, S. (1998) *Who Moved My Cheese?* New York: Putnum Adult.

Oppong, T. (2017) 'Getting Stuck is Not a Problem. Staying Stuck is', *Medium*, April [Online]. Availabe at: https://medium.com/personal-growth/getting-stuck-is-not-a-problem-staying-stuck-is-d8c747889619 (accessed 6 November 2020).

Sizzle Podcast (2019) Iesha Small [The Unexpected Leader] #012, 8 April [Online]. Available at: https://anchor.fm/thesizzlepodcast/episodes/012-Iesha-Small-The-Unexpected-Leader-e3l4jq (accessed 12 July 2020).

Yusuf, B. (2017) 'Stepping into leadership and identifying your core values', *Leadership Matters*, 12 June [Online]. Available at: www.leadershipmatters.org.uk/articles/stepping-into-leadership-and-identifying-your-core-values (accessed 23 October 2019).

32
INSPIRING THE FUTURE
Vivienne Porritt

KEY POINTS

This chapter will:

- Show why it is important to support young women's ambition;
- Remind us that many women experience self-doubt which needs tackling;
- Insist that women's voices are heard in education;
- Highlight inclusive leadership.

INTRODUCTION

I congratulate all our chapter authors for sharing their stories of being 10% braver. They have also been brave to offer advice to help you tackle imposter syndrome, negotiate your salary or flexible working, to ask for what you need, to call out unacceptable behaviour, to put yourself first when necessary and, perhaps, for women in education, the bravest ask of all: 'knowing your worth' (Porritt, 2019a).

The #WomenEd *community* has written this book so that you can draw on valuable advice to tackle some of the situations described. I am also concerned that the next generation of female educators and leaders may have to tackle the same issues. This is why #WomenEd wants to break the cycle of inequality in leadership roles, salary, professional support and the motherhood penalty. If this book achieves the purpose of inspiring existing female leaders to be 10% braver, we must also *challenge* and *change* the way our future female leaders are identified and developed. A huge thank you to the wonderful members of our #WomenEd *community* who offered the suggestions in this chapter to inspire the next generation of women to lead education.

IDENTIFYING ASPIRING LEADERS

Existing leaders, both women and men, need to be proactive in seeking out early career teachers with ambitions to be leaders. We need to work alongside them, mentor and then coach them. Most importantly, we need to plan a leadership pathway with them. Rather than corralling this as an interview question, let's ask women early in their career where they see themselves in five years. Positive *challenge* at this point can help women to be ambitious with their personal plan. An allocated mentor can then help to put steps in place to achieve leadership goals. A tweet saddened me: 'I wanted to be a leader since my NQT year and had to make it up/work out what to do, implement and pay for it myself' (Slater, 2019a).

Whatever form of appraisal is conducted, leaders need to ensure we are more 'deliberate and really act quite urgently if we want to *change* the landscape of leadership. When we see potential, we need to chase these folks down!' (Hannay, 2019).

So, middle and senior leaders need to seek out those women who want to lead or clearly have the capacity to lead, and guide them to achieve their leadership goals. Is such an approach part of your leadership development plans currently? Raise these points with senior leaders and governors if not.

I think everyone has doubts, but many women allow their doubts to hold themselves back. Add perfectionism and imposter syndrome into the mix, as we have read in these chapters, and we have young women who, as Hillary Clinton has pointed out, 'are harder on themselves than circumstances warrant. They are too often selling themselves short' (Bennett, 2014).

Interestingly, some respondents highlighted the value of having doubts and even imposter syndrome, saying they would rather follow a leader who was able to voice their doubts and ask for alternative views than one with no doubts at all.

The #WomenEd *community* is very clear on this issue. We need to be authentic in vocalising our doubts, set them against our considerable achievements and seek to make the most of support from those around us. This is at the heart of what we want our *community* to achieve. Strong role models (both female and male) are essential to inspire the next generation and these role models need to share their stories of both success and 'failing forward', as we learn in Chapter 26. Such role models, as well as mentors and coaches, must be willing to trust you, advocate for you and have your back if things go wrong.

BEING HEARD

As a young teacher I have struggled with the idea of how to be heard best and how to sell myself. One thing I've learnt is you have to do it your way not copy others! (Longhurst, 2019)

This is a perennial problem and women's voices in education need to be heard more. Jill Berry offers words of wisdom for this: 'It's about being assertive, I think, and avoiding apologetic language which can actually diminish what you are saying' (Berry, 2019).

When I run workshops on this topic, women share the kind of language that diminishes them. It's a cathartic experience and we work on replacing what they say with more direct and clear language. Apologising unnecessarily doesn't make us seem pleasant; it can make (male) colleagues think we're weak and so they stop listening: such linguistic differences have a tangible impact. Subjective views of men and women vary enormously, with women far more likely to be described as 'indecisive, inept and panicky' (Smith et al., 2018). The thing is, 'we are experts in our fields and it's sad that we sometimes feel the need to make ourselves smaller in the eyes of other people' (Porritt, 2019b). Let's put learning about the effective use of language on the agenda for early career teachers, so that they can stop unconsciously sabotaging themselves and communicate courageously and authentically.

Equally, it's vital that existing educational leaders play their part in supporting women's voices to be heard. How would your organisation respond to this statement?

> [A]s a young female teacher I didn't voice my aspirations to be a leader for fear of rejection. No one ever asked me either. Which compounded my view that no one believed I was capable. If leaders asked, maybe women would get better at voicing their ambitions. (Slater, 2019b)

The action here is clear. Senior leaders need to seek out opportunities to enable women to have a voice and act upon what is said. And if we want girls to be the leaders of tomorrow, their teachers and leaders need to be role models in showing that women's voices are important and are heard.

INCLUSIVE LEADERSHIP

An issue that exercises our *community* significantly is what happens to women who are leaders, step away from their role to have a family and then look to return to a leadership position. Many women do not climb the traditional career ladder as quickly or as straightforwardly as men and we discuss this at length in *10% Braver: Inspiring Women to Lead Education* (Porritt and Featherstone, 2019).

Another group of women we need to support and encourage are women who were middle or senior leaders, even headteachers, and who reduced hours or left to have a family and who then return to education. Many find it difficult to gain leadership posts and we hear of interview questions asking whether they are serious about developing as a leader again. What can your organisation do for someone in this situation?

Such questions could be indicative of unconscious bias, and however well meaning the question might be, do take care to ask all candidates the same questions and avoid potentially biased follow-up questions.

In a severe recruitment and retention crisis, women with existing experience of leadership need to be inspired to return, and be valued for their experience and expertise. How can we ensure more women are able to finish their leadership story in this way?

In another example, 'The proportion of teachers aged 50 or over [in England] has fallen from 23 per cent in 2010 to just 17 per cent in 2017' (Worth, 2018). We seem to be leaking both women who have a family and experienced teachers and leaders in their fifties and older. This is at a time when the pensionable age for women educators keeps increasing and 'Some of us now feel too old as leaders get younger – those who went part time due to circumstances now feel we missed the boat!' (Smith, 2019).

That boat is far too leaky if women also hear this: 'I was told last year by my HT that if I didn't apply for SLT soon I'd miss the boat entirely and have opted myself out of leadership as most SLT these days are very young. I'm 45 with decades left in my career' (Cruikshanks, 2019).

We must support experienced women to share their expertise. Instead of throwing them overboard, they can encourage, support, develop, coach, inspire and lead the next generation of women leaders.

Sarah Mullin hits the nail on the head:

> The denial of gender bias by men and women, including those who may have experienced gender related prejudice, is described as the 'no-problem, problem' (Rhode, 1991). It is essential that the existence of gender discrimination is acknowledged so that positive steps can be taken to overcome the barriers to leadership. (Mullin, personal *communication*, 5 December 2019)

We ask existing female and male leaders to look at the ways they enable women's voices to be heard and how they develop future women leaders so they can lead education.

We ask individual women educators to consider this advice from Sarah Wynn:

> Don't be afraid to push yourself out of your comfort zone. Sometimes opportunities can appear overwhelming and out of your remit of expertise, but just remember that the *challenge* makes goals even more obtainable, because you're committed and determined to succeed. (Wynn, personal *communication*, 5 December 2019)

Kate Corbin wants to tell women to 'go for it, not underestimate themselves and recognise how brilliant' they are (Corbin, personal *communication*, 4 December 2019).

There is no better way to close than with words from the inimitable Jill Berry:

> We need to build girls' and women's *confidence* in their own capacity, to ensure they give themselves full credit for what they have achieved in the past, and what they may be able to accomplish in the future. Recognise leadership is challenging but it can also be hugely rewarding and joyful. (Berry, personal *communication*, 4 December 2019)

Brilliant leaders are needed globally. The #WomenEd *community* is here to support and empower you and we've got your back. Now is the time for women to step up as leaders by being 10% braver.

Passing on being 10% braver

- Be deliberate in finding women educators who want to or have the capacity to lead and help them plan their leadership path.
- *Challenge* the organisational approach to developing leaders so there are specific opportunities for women.
- Raise your voice until it is heard.
- Ask for the support and development you want and, remember, it's never too late to be 10% braver.

REFERENCES

Bennett, J. (2014) 'It's not you, it's science: How perfectionism holds women back', *Time*, 22 April [Online]. Available at: https://time.com/70558/its-not-you-its-science-how-perfectionism-holds-women-back (accessed 3 April 2020).

Berry, J. [@jillberry102] (2019) 5 December [Twitter]. Available at: https://twitter.com/jillberry102/status/1202617425746964482?s=20 (accessed 3 April 2020).

Cruickshanks, K. [@mscruickers] (2019) 8 December [Twitter]. Available at: https://twitter.com/mscruickers/status/1203584208742039552?s=20 (accessed 6 April 2020).

Hannay, L. [@lhannay1] (2019) 4 December [Twitter]. Available at: https://twitter.com/lhannay1/status/1202219838187327488?s=20 (accessed 5 April 2020).

Longhurst, E. [emmalonhurst64] (2019) 5 December [Twitter]. Available at: https://twitter.com/emmalonghurst64/status/1202615302464380928?s=20 (accessed 3 April 2020).

Porritt, V. (2019a) 'How to negotiate a higher salary as a teacher, *tes*, 11 August [Online]. Available at: www.tes.com/news/pay-interview-how-negotiate-higher-salary-teacher (accessed 5 August 2020).

Porritt, V. (2019b) 'Women, we've got to stop saying sorry at work', *tes*, 25 December [Online]. Available at: www.tes.com/news/women-weve-got-stop-saying-sorry-work (accessed 4 April 2020)

Porritt, V. and Featherstone, K. (eds) (2019) *10% Braver: Inspiring Women to Lead Education*. London: Sage.

Rhode, D. L. (1991) 'The "no-problem" problem: Feminist *challenges* and cultural *change*', *Yale Law Journal*, 100: 1731–93 [Online]. Available at: https://digitalcommons.law.yale.edu/cgi/viewcontent.cgi?article=7350&context=ylj (accessed 7 April 2020).

Slater, K. [@southwestsenco] (2019a) 4 December [Twitter]. Available at: https://twitter.com/southwestsenco/status/1202112412964605952?s=20 (accessed 5 April 2010).

Slater, K. [@southwestsenco] (2019b) 4 December [Twitter] Available at: https://twitter.com/southwestsenco/status/1202280000625479681?s=20 (accessed 5 April 2020).

Smith, D. G., Rosenstein, J. E. and Nikolov, C. (2018) 'The different words we use to describe male and female leaders', *Harvard Business Review*, 25 May [Online]. Available at: https://hbr.org/2018/05/the-different-words-we-use-to-describe-male-and-female-leaders%20-%20Smith,%20Rosenstein,%20Nicolov (accessed 3 April 2020).

Smith, E. [@MadgiePodge] (2019) 7 December [Twitter] Available at: https://twitter.com/MadgiePodge/status/1203318831864782854?s=20 (accessed 6 April 2020).

Worth, J. (2018) 'Latest teacher retention statistics paint a bleak picture for teacher supply in England', *NFER*, 28 June [Online]. Available at: www.nfer.ac.uk/news-events/nfer-blogs/latest-teacher-retention-statistics-paint-a-bleak-picture-for-teacher-supply-in-england (accessed 6 April 2010).

INDEX